Firefighters

in the

Hot Seat

Firefighters
in the
Hot Seat

A FIREFIGHTER'S GUIDE TO OPS INVESTIGATIONS

Lance J. LoRusso, Esq.

BOOKLOGIX®

Alpharetta, GA

ISBN: 978-1-61005-967-1 - Paperback
eISBN: 978-1-61005-968-8 - ePub
eISBN: 978-1-61005-969-5 - mobi

Library of Congress Control Number: 2020909491

Printed in the United States of America   0 5 2 6 2 0

☉This paper meets the requirements of ANSI/NISO Z39.48-1992 (Permanence of Paper)

This book is dedicated to the brave women and men who put on the uniform and step into the gap to attain the title of "Firefighter." Their backgrounds are as varied as the environments and conditions in which they work. Some face danger in areas prone to earthquakes and forest fires, while others confront the hazardous reality of being a public safety officer in high-crime areas most people would not enter on a bet—with their car doors and windows locked up tight.

They answer a call they hear in their hearts, not on the radio or on a speaker in the station. Their saves are never forgotten by those who have one more Christmas or Thanksgiving with their families, the dad who survives a heart attack to one day walk his daughter down the aisle, and the child hiding under a bed in a burning house only to see an angel in turnout gear change the course of a family's history.

We remember always those who risk their lives for strangers every day. We pray every night for their safety, and we will never forget those who answered the call and never returned home.

When a man becomes a fireman
his greatest act of bravery has been accomplished.
What he does after that is all in the line of work.

—Chief Edward F. Croker
New York Fire Department

CONTENTS

DISCLAIMER

Nothing in this book should be construed as legal advice. When an attorney gives legal advice, a client or potential client provides specific facts and the attorney analyzes and considers those facts to craft a plan tailored to the situation.

The sample documents included in this book are for demonstrative purposes only. Do not use them to defend or appeal discipline in your specific case. I am including them to illustrate what those documents contain and hopefully remove the fear and mystery of the language if you are ever reading one while under the stress of an investigation.

The front-line stories are fictionalized accounts of cases my firm has handled, that have appeared in the news, or of which I am personally aware. They are included to give both context and reference to the reader. Remember that the accounts and facts have been manipulated to preserve anonymity and privacy. However, the discipline and the stress of that process was real for the firefighters involved. Perhaps by learning of their stories, you will be better able and motivated to defend yourself if, or when, you are in the hot seat.

The information in this book is intended to be, and is in fact, generic. My intent is to take some of the fear out of the unknown and to encourage every reader to develop a plan that includes contacting and consulting with an attorney if you find yourself the subject of an internal or administrative investigation. You take a big risk attempting to face such an investigation alone and without the advice and support of competent counsel. The potential loss of pay, standing, professional licensure, and your career are certainly worth the money and time it takes to seek professional counsel.

FOREWORD

From the first day of recruit school, firefighters are taught to function in teams and never leave their partner. Whether advancing a hoseline down a hallway to a burning room, searching a smoke-filled second floor, or building a complex rope system to lower someone over the side of a building to make a rescue, the partner concept provides a level of safety, confidence, and trust that only those in high-risk professions understand. We spend hours training for these events and would never consider going it alone in any Immediately Dangerous to Life and Health (IDLH) environment. We always have each other's backs.

The dedicated public servant considers what we do a calling and not a job. We sacrifice to do what we love, often for low pay, long erratic hours, some decent benefits, old equipment, crumbling facilities, and lots of bureaucracy, all for that chance to help a stranger in need. We often assume that no matter what happens, our departments will have our backs. We know we will make mistakes, but operate under a pretense that as long as we are doing our best, our chiefs will understand and support us. Unfortunately, many departments have become riddled with leaders who operate under a philosophy of plausible deniability.

As firefighters, we want to work in well-disciplined and orderly organizations. If someone violates their oath of office, we want them to be held accountable. During my eight years as a firefighter union president, I represented dozens of firefighters and officers during investigations, discipline, and civil service hearings. I told each one the same thing: if you are guilty, I will do everything I can to make sure your rights are protected and you get a fair investigation and process—but I can't defend you. If you are innocent, I will do the same and vigorously defend you against the allegations.

Speaking generally about the state of fire and EMS departments around the United States, too often our firefighters find themselves the subject of complaints filed by bad bosses who are not trained in how to lead, manage, or motivate employees. They use the department's disciplinary process as a safe space to place the burden on someone else in the organization so they won't have to deal with a situation that requires leadership. During my eight years representing employees, only 20 percent of the cases warranted the time the department put into them. The rest were the result of personality conflicts, ego, or payback for something done earlier in a career, because the accuser had rank over them.

If you are a good employee, love your job, stay up to date on training, and help out where and whenever you can, you expect that you will probably never have to deal with any type of internal investigation. Well, you are wrong. The more you do for an organization, the more out there you are, the more chances you have for making a mistake. The more you stand out, the more you will be scrutinized and attacked by some. I know it doesn't make sense that a guy can do absolutely nothing for the organization other than show up for work and never get in any type of trouble. Unfortunately, that is the world we live in, and bad things can happen to good people. When they do, you will have a tendency to think the department will look out for your best interests, consider your previous work, and have your back. But unless you are working for that unicorn organization, you are likely wrong.

Consider any internal investigation an Immediately Dangerous to Lifestyle and Career (IDLC) environment and never go it alone. You have rights. You need a partner who knows what those rights are and who can guide you through the process. You should always have an employee representative, union representative, or attorney with you at all proceedings. Obviously, the circumstances will dictate the level of investment you make. There is no need to spend thousands of dollars to prevent a letter of counseling for being late to work—especially if you were late. Take responsibility and move on. On the other hand, you need to know the maximum potential levels of discipline for the violation you are being accused of. If it represents a substantial loss of money, rank, eligibility for future promotion, or termination, then you should build your team to protect yourself, your family, and your career!

No one wants to spend hours studying and preparing for the "what-if" scenario of being under investigation. We want to spend our time getting better at our craft so that when called upon, we can perform and make the rescue, save the life, and minimize harm. That is exactly why, just as when conducting a search, you should never go it alone. You will need a partner who has experience in an area in which you have little, if any. Asking for expert help is not a sign of weakness.

Lance J. LoRusso, Esq., has put together a highly condensed body of work to give you an awareness level of your rights as well as some guiding principles to follow should you find yourself caught "in the hot seat" of your administration or a bad boss. Even if you did something that warrants action by your department, you still have rights and should expect a fair process and that the action taken against you will be consistent with past decisions and appropriate for the violation.

Lance blends both technical and historical legal precedent with real examples and laymen translations into how these things apply to you. He does this with the perspective only a person who has served on the street as a public servant could have. If you plan on making the fire service your career, you need to read and follow the guidance offered in this book. This should also be required reading for any officer or chief in the fire service. Understanding that your members have rights and that you can't just handle these situations based on emotion will go a long way in keeping you from needing an attorney to defend against your former employee!

—David Rhodes
Nationally Recognized Expert in Firefighting
Chief Elder, Georgia Smoke Diver Association
Thirty-Four Years of Service

ACKNOWLEDGMENTS

Many thanks to my colleague Hayden Hillyer, Esq., former police officer, for his assistance in researching the laws and citations for this book.

Many thanks also to the men and women in the fire service who have shared their stories and permitted me the honor of representing them.

INTRODUCTION

You will never do anything in this world without courage.
It is the greatest quality of the mind next to honor.

— Aristotle

I remember the first time a firefighter asked me for help. It was a simple case of policy being applied in, quite frankly, a silly manner. He was convinced the proposed discipline was inappropriate, but his chain of command thought otherwise. In writing for both sides to see, was a set of policies that held the answer. Once the lawyers got involved, the situation resolved quickly and with little aggravation. Then the lawyers stepped away to another case, and the firefighter was left to work with those same supervisors and managers, who had to backtrack to comply with policy. I left the firefighter in a better place, facing a bright career and future, and with my cell phone number, because I knew I would likely hear from him again.

There is a basic disconnect in the fire service between

firefighters working on the street answering calls and some managers who have not worked in a station for decades. A lot of people forget, or conveniently ignore, a simple fact: firefighters work in conditions that will not fit into a manual. Even if every situation could be addressed in policy, no one would have time to read it when seconds count and lives are in the balance. You, the reader, and all those in this honored profession, must make judgment calls, and that means you will make mistakes. When mistakes occur, you must remember that state and federal due process rights, specific rights set out in city charters, collective bargaining agreements, policies, and personnel manuals mean something. They are not just window dressing. Sometimes firefighters are exonerated, and sometimes they must face the consequences of poor decisions. However, in all cases, you are entitled to be treated fairly and according to the law.

Despite the dangers of the job, nothing can be more stressful than a call to report to the chief's office. The email, phone call, or memo that communicates this information can make even the toughest firefighter queasy. *What do they want? What did I do now? Is there a complaint brewing? What supervisor is mad about something? What did someone else do that I'm caught up in?* These questions and more fill the mind in an instant. A trip to the Office of Professional Standards (OPS) has the same effect—or worse.

For the purposes of this book, I am using the title "Office of Professional Standards," or OPS, as a common term to describe the division of the fire department or government entity that conducts internal or administrative investigations. Some agencies call this division "Internal Affairs," the "Office of Professional Responsibility," or "Inspector General." They all operate in the same manner, for the most part. They are tasked with conducting investigations involving violations of policy, state or federal law, and codes of conduct through a process typically internal to the agency.

The purpose of this book is to take some of the mystery out of those calls, to convince you that such a call should not put more fear in your heart than penetrating a structure fire looking for survivors, and to urge you to be prepared for that call, as it will likely come at least once in your career. Like any other call, advanced preparation is the key to success—and survival. Fire departments are run by people with personalities, egos, biases, and belief systems. Like the firefighters they supervise and manage, they will make mistakes. Some fall victim to political influence and a desire for personal gain. This is to say they are human. Sometimes they will perform heroically, and other times they will fail. The difference, many times, means a person in their charge may suffer terrible and sometimes irreversible injury.

In the course of my law practice, I have routinely

accompanied firefighters to OPS interviews. Some of those interviews pertained to minor policy violations. Others involved allegations of serious misconduct and violations of state and federal law. In every case, we meet with our clients, review the facts, review the applicable policies, procedures, laws, or incident reports, and ensure they are properly prepared to answer questions. I have tremendous respect for firefighters, and I hate to see the people who put their lives at risk for strangers afraid that they will not be treated fairly by their own departments.

In the United States, 1,056,200[1] people have earned the title of firefighter. I have been fortunate to have met engineers, lieutenants, captains, battalion chiefs, deputy chiefs, and chiefs who will still tell you they are firefighters when you ask what they do. Although many professions claim to be in touch with their roots and history, firefighters' connection with the legacy of those who came before them is evident from the traditions that survive today and the commitment to public service that has been passed down for generations.

Speaking of generations, no public service is more steeped in family tradition than the fire service. Perhaps it is because many police departments foolishly put in place nepotistic policies for many years that prevented husbands and wives, as well as sons and daughters, from getting a paycheck from the same government.

Fortunately, it appears that many of those antiquated policies are fading into history.

This book will address internal investigations of firefighters irrespective of their rank, role, duties, or status as paid or volunteer. Having represented many firefighters of virtually all ranks and titles facing internal investigations and discipline, I am constantly amazed at how petty and absurd some of those investigations truly are. While I have certainly been involved in serious, well-founded inquiries into true misconduct, many times the firefighter in my office is facing discipline over something trivial that never should have risen to any level of investigation. All too often, the proposed discipline involves a loss of pay without consideration for any other method to change or correct behavior, even when an oral or written reprimand would deter the conduct in the future.

Why write a book about firefighter discipline? That's a simple answer. A large part of my mission through my firm is to support the public safety heroes who put everything on the line, often their very lives and health, to save and rescue strangers. One of my pet peeves is that those very same firefighters, who will run into a burning building, approach a burning car, or volunteer as SWAT medics to save lives while literally under fire, will endure real, life-changing stress at the hands of a heavy-handed or unscrupulous supervisor. Anything

I can do to reduce that stress would make this book a success.

You will notice I have included notes throughout this book—the small numbers you see occasionally in the text—that correspond to numbered items in the Notes section at the end of the book. These notes provide information about references, resource materials, and details that can be helpful to further expand on a topic and sometimes give more legal-ese for those so inclined to delve deeper into a topic. Use them as you will.

I hope this book will take some of the mystery out of the OPS and disciplinary processes and convince you that advanced preparation is imperative. I will not use fear tactics in this book like a lot of trainers and authors do. Having been the subject of internal investigations, I know the experience will be scary enough. This book is *not* a manual for how to handle an OPS case without an attorney. I structured this book to build your knowledge base as I walk you through the steps of an OPS investigation. At the end, if you have not convinced yourself that you should carefully consider hiring an attorney at the first inkling you are under investigation, then you are reading the wrong book. OPS and discipline cases are complex, challenging procedural exercises where the career of a dedicated firefighter hangs in the balance. Don't go it alone.

Chapter 1

Why Are Firefighters Caught in the Hot Seat?

*Firefighting is different. I mean, you live with
the people you work with. Most people can't
wait to leave the office at the end of the day.
At the end of a stressful call, we go back to
the station with our crew. Some we would
choose as best friends. Others we would not.*

—Anonymous

Firefighters responded to 36,750,000 calls for service in 2018. Of those, only 1,318,500 were fires. At 23,551,500, the majority were medical calls, and 2,899,000 were false alarms.[2] Today's firefighter faces dangers from natural disasters, violent criminals, and the stress that comes from responding to some of the worst events in our society. As you know, even false alarms carry all of the same stress as true emergencies. Still, they respond, work with the resources available to them, and stay focused on the mission.

You won't find a database that tells you the number of OPS investigations done on firefighters every year, or the number of firefighters who are investigated or written up for discipline at the command level. I suspect there are two reasons for this. First, no one tracks those statistics. Second, no one really wants the truth to come out. However, ask any union representative, seasoned firefighter, or attorney who represents firefighters and they will tell you how much time they spend dealing with investigations and discipline.

Why do firefighters find themselves dealing with so many OPS investigations and disciplinary actions? Having handled many of them, here are my thoughts on six possibilities.

1. Stress
2. Firefighter Culture

3. Fatigue and Financial Pressure
4. Exposure to Human Suffering
5. Improper Discipline
6. Improper Training

Stress

Sometimes investigations arise as a by-product of the very nature of firefighting. Work-related stress can lead to unpleasant and even horrible interactions. An off-handed or passing comment, quickly dismissed in any other environment, may create a conflict in an environment where the stakes are high, tempers are short, and coworkers are fatigued.

Firefighter Culture

Firefighters spend a lot of time together. The very foundation of firefighting culture is a dispatch-and-response system predicated upon units responding twenty-four hours each day from central locations. Unlike law enforcement, firefighters do not "patrol" while waiting for a dispatch. This model causes people with varied personalities, backgrounds, and belief systems to not only work together on twenty-four-hour shifts, but also live together.

I have represented several firefighters who were the subject of rumors. While every employment environment has its share of rumors, in a firefighter's world the rumors never get a break when the "office" is closed. The rumors spread from one shift to another and get passed around twenty-four hours each day, every day. They climb the chain of command, and like the fires they fight, rumors about firefighters jump the lines from one agency to another. In more than one instance, I represented firefighters who were reported to OPS for allegations of misconduct by the command staff of neighboring agencies when the rumors began within the firefighter's own agency. The rumors were, like most, largely untrue or exaggerated. However, there was nothing imagined or fictional about the OPS investigation, the administrative leave pending the outcome of the investigation, or the toll the investigation took on my clients or those who were interviewed by OPS, including their spouses. In the end, they were cleared. However, the allegations left a cloud over the firefighters and a severe breach of trust in their wake. At least one left their agency, and one left the profession.

 FRONT-LINE STORY

I represented a firefighter who was accused of infidelity with another firefighter's spouse. By the time the

rumor made it around the department, the firefighter was reportedly sleeping with a dozen women. He was cleared, but the stigma and the jokes continued. He went from being a great, motivated employee to one counting the days until retirement.

Fatigue and Financial Pressure

Fatigue and financial pressures are real in the fire service, and public safety in general. The average hourly pay of a firefighter is $25.60.[3] While there can be a large variation, with the highest-paid firefighter receiving $42.75[4] per hour, firefighters are paid far less than people believe, and far less than would be required if recruits and incumbents were not motivated by a higher calling. Because of these wages, many firefighters, in my experience, work more than one full-time job, have a company they run in their "off hours," or work as much overtime as they can. Although the typical full-time schedule of a firefighter allows time for additional work, somewhere in that "extra" time, the firefighter must squeeze in family time, sleep, and some fun! No one will dispute that fatigued employees make more errors and are more susceptible to the stressors of close living quarters.

Exposure to Human Suffering

Firefighting often involves dealing with horrible injuries, destruction, devastation, and death. A recent news story I read recognized this fact when the reporter remarked she was struck that the firefighters on the scene had described the damage as the worst they had ever encountered. No matter how strong you are, no matter how you've learned to distance yourself from the suffering of others, that type of exposure to human suffering takes its toll. We have represented firefighters suffering from depression, post-traumatic stress (PTS), post-traumatic stress disorder (PTSD),[5] alcohol and drug dependence, severe insomnia, and anxiety. Left untreated or unaddressed, such conditions will surface and manifest themselves as "discipline issues," which can begin as minor offenses such as tardiness, or more serious offenses such as arrests for impaired driving. Unfortunately, without involved, educated, and caring leadership taught to recognize and address these warning signs, even minor violations often lead to termination under a progressive discipline policy.[6]

Unfortunately, without involved, educated, and caring leadership taught to recognize and address these warning signs, even minor violations often lead to termination under a progressive discipline policy.

Improper Discipline

All too often, the public sector sees suspension and termination as a first-level tool to solve every problem. In the conclusion of this book, you will find an article entitled "10 Steps to Lowering the Rate of Public Sector Discipline and Avoiding Lawsuits," which I wrote for PoliceOne.com appearing on March 6, 2019. The wide, favorable response to this article was flattering. However, the comments were disheartening. All too often the readers responded that they wished their chain of command, supervisors, or government leaders would read the article and learn something. We have seen discipline that was, quite frankly, just plain silly. Other times, we were dealing with a chief who got his feelings hurt or refused to admit he was wrong. In both cases, the effect on morale was devastating and irreversible. In my humble opinion, there is too much at stake to make discipline anything other than a last resort. Each time I teach employment law at the Georgia Command College at Columbus State University, I always tell student-leaders on the first day that they should never fire or discipline anyone when they are tired or angry. I also encourage training as an alternative to discipline. It's hard for someone to appeal or sue over mandatory training, and if your agency is properly screening applicants, you should want to do everything possible to keep the people you hired and trained.

HOT TIP

Never fire or discipline anyone when you are tired or angry, and instead of discipline, try offering training instead. It's hard for someone to appeal or sue over mandatory training.

Improper Training

Most errors in the workplace are the result of improper training, poor supervision, bad policies, or poor communication. However, addressing those issues head on requires the people in command, all the way down, to utter three words that, to some, are worse than having a tooth pulled: *I was wrong.* Training and communication are essential. If the same violations appear repeatedly or are pervasive throughout a division or department, look to training and communication deficiencies or the policy itself. If the same supervisor seems to have issues with firefighters making the same or a lot of errors, perhaps the problem is the supervisor. This type of analysis helps the agency. I've never heard of anyone successfully suing an agency or government entity because they

Most errors in the workplace are the result of improper training, poor supervision, bad policies, or poor communication.

were trained too much. Supervision and management of an agency requires more than just monitoring statistics on performance. The intentional analysis of statistics regarding discipline will identify problem employees, deficient training, inconsistently applied or poorly worded policies, or bad supervisors and managers. All are detrimental and must be addressed.

I make a lot of suggestions in this chapter that would likely reduce the incidence of discipline among firefighters, make a lot of agencies better places to work, and make the firefighters working there better, more efficient, and a lot happier. Unfortunately, I do not believe we will see a lot of changes in these areas. So, firefighters need to be prepared to personally deal with discipline and OPS investigations when they arise. You worked too hard to enter this profession to have it taken from you unjustly.

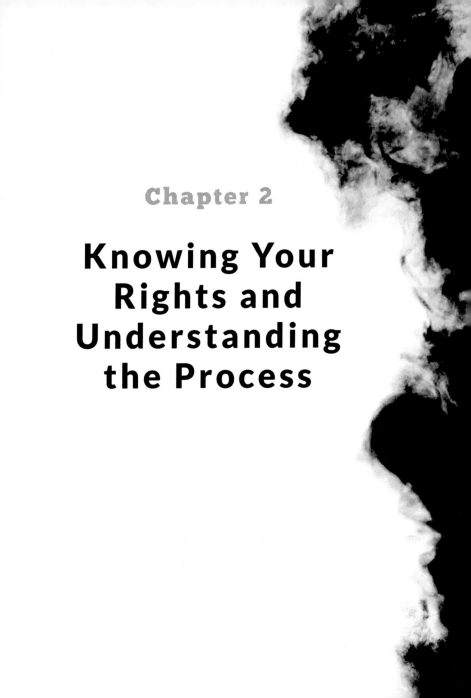

Chapter 2

Knowing Your Rights and Understanding the Process

"Before I knew it, I went from working
a shift to administrative leave."

"In a week, I was interviewed, investigated,
and recommended for discipline."

"I had no idea they could do that or what my rights
were. I was scrambling to find an attorney and
read the policies that now affected my career."

—Quotes from several firefighter clients

The most frightening question I receive from clients facing an administrative investigation is, "Do I have any rights?" I truly hate to hear these words. They tell me first that the firefighter feels helpless. Second, the words convey that the firefighter is not aware of the policies and procedures in their own department that ensure they will be treated fairly. This question usually arises from a lack of education, which ultimately falls back on the department.[7] It usually also indicates a level of distrust of management. Both indicate a sad state of affairs. If you are a supervisor, work hard to eliminate both situations. If you are in senior management, commit to eliminate this type of uncertainty. It only serves to put a cloud of suspicion on what may be a legitimate disciplinary process.

Back to the original question: "Do I have any rights?" Not to "lawyer up" on you, but it depends. The good news is, it is relatively easy to answer that question *before* you are ordered to report to OPS! Appendix A contains a Sample Notice of Investigation. The stress you will experience upon receiving a letter like this will consume you. That is the wrong time to start searching policy manuals, ordinances, and other materials to learn about your rights and the appeal process.

The reality is that some of you reading this book will have more rights than

"Do I have any rights?" Not to "lawyer up" on you, but it depends.

others. The levels of appeal and rights afforded to you, and in fact whether you have these at all, depends in large part on the area in which you work, because state laws vary greatly regarding employee rights. All of you work for a government, and whether it is a state, county, or city entity who provides your paycheck, that government passes laws and policies that control its relationship with employees.

There are instances in which a contract is formed between the firefighter and her employer, called a collective bargaining agreement. This contract sets out the obligations and rights of the parties, and the terms are generally enforceable in court. In other instances, some firefighters will sign individual contracts with their employers, although these are relatively rare. Finally, as a citizen or a person subject to the jurisdiction of the United States, you have rights under both the United States Constitution and your state constitution. This may sound complicated, and it can be. All the more reason to learn the ropes before you step into the ring and to be prepared to use the services of an attorney familiar with these areas if you find yourself in the arena. Because you are generally permitted to handle these matters with an attorney, you should carefully consider that strategy. If you decide to hire an attorney, look for an attorney or firm that actually litigates cases in court. Every hearing, no matter how informal, is serious. Our firm is made up of litigators. If you are searching for a firm in your state or region, review their website to examine their experience with litigation and handling OPS matters.

So again, back to the original question: "Do I have any rights?" Let's look at the five typical sources of rights and protection firefighters can look to when they face discipline:

1. Rights Arising from Policies and Ordinances
2. State Law
3. City Charters
4. Collective Bargaining Agreements
5. Employment Contracts
6. Due Process Clauses of Federal and State Constitutions

Rights Arising from Policies and Ordinances

Irrespective of any state or federal law, a department or government entity can give you rights through a policy, ordinance, and/or other documents that control how the government entity runs. Therefore, your search for rights should begin with the policy manual for your department and the government entity that employs you. These are two separate documents. Every government entity has a set of policies, and while those policies are usually the same as those in your department, sometimes they can be far broader and more detailed. In fact, your department policy manual will likely refer you to the main government policy manual. We have represented clients who found rights in their government manual that were not set out clearly or at all in their department policies.

 HOT TIP

Obtain copies of both your department policy manual and the government policy manual, and read them NOW *before you are in the hot seat!*

Ordinances often describe how the government entity functions. They may cover everything from zoning to personnel. It is important to remember that a city or county performs legislative actions just like a state or the federal government. For this reason, those ordinances are said to "have the force of law" and may control or take precedence if the policies of the government entity are silent or ambiguous.[8] You can find these ordinances in a few places. Many government entities publish their ordinances online at www.municode.com. You can also go to the website for your county or city clerk. Finally, you can always ask for a copy at the clerk's office. Be sure to ask for only the personnel or other specific ordinances. The complete code of ordinances may be a foot thick or take up more than two volumes.

Once you locate those policies and ordinances, make certain you keep a copy handy. If you are a union representative or a supervisor, you owe a duty to your troops to have a copy available. In my experience, administrative investigations arise very quickly with little notice. Do not wait until you are under the stress of a pending investigation to search for these policies. Have a copy available to you.

Now that you've found them, *read them!* Do not rely upon someone in the human resources department or the chief's office to tell you what those policies actually say. I have seen dozens of situations when the "interpretation" from the person who reportedly knew what the policy or ordinance set out was, well, completely wrong. This is critical with appeals. If you do not follow the policy on appeals to the letter or miss a deadline, you may lose all rights to appeal the discipline at issue.

Some of these policies read well. They are clear, concise, cover only one subject, and are written to inform, educate, and provide guidance. Others . . . are different. In short, they are terribly written. I'm fairly fluent in English, have a master's degree, and graduated law school with honors. However, I confess that I have read policies that made little, if any, sense. I have also found policies that made me feel like an ancient explorer navigating uncharted territories, because no one in the agency or government entity knew what the policies set out or how to follow them.

 FRONT-LINE STORY

Several years ago, I helped a LEO[9] appeal his termination from a small city police department. We lost the first level of appeal before the mayor. No surprise, as the mayor had approved the termination initially. So, we filed an appeal to the next level, which was a hearing before the "Public Safety Committee." When I didn't hear anything about our appeal for several weeks, I called the city attorney for a status update. He explained the reason for the delay: no one knew my client had another level of appeal. Further, they had no idea who made up this "Public Safety Committee." Amazing. We got his termination reversed at that level. I was excited, but also a bit disappointed to conclude the adventure. There would have been another level of appeal if we lost. I can only imagine how another appeal up the chain would have shaken up that little town, and there's no telling who would have been on that next committee!

Policies are important. The agency and the department put them together, voted on them, and implemented them. That means they must follow them. For example, I've been able to push for the dismissal of discipline simply because it was instituted outside the bounds of the time period set out in the policy.

Here are some other reasons I have been able to challenge discipline using the language of a departmental or government policy:

- The discipline was not handled properly through the correct chain of command.
- The appropriate individuals did not "sign off" on the findings of fact or the recommended discipline.
- The government entity failed to schedule or hold a hearing within the prescribed time limits.
- The department failed to follow the discipline "schedule" when selecting a punishment, or "overcharged" the employee based upon the facts.
- The employee was not properly advised of their rights.
- The employee was not provided proper notice of the allegations or charges.
- The conduct of the employee did not violate any policies, laws, or conduct codes.[10]

- The employee was not provided sufficient time to prepare for the administrative interview.
- The government entity failed to comply with the applicable open records act to provide relevant documents to us to prepare for the hearing and subpoena witnesses.
- The investigation failed to follow all of the procedures set out in the applicable policy.
- The policy did not conform with state law or conflicted with the constitutional rights of the employee.

Have I convinced you yet of the importance of searching for, reading, and keeping handy a copy of the applicable policies? This may also cause your organization or union to push for changes to these policies to better protect firefighters in the department before a conflict arises.

Finally, department or government policies may establish civil service, personnel boards, or some other body that reviews discipline based upon an appeal from the employee. Some of these entities are established by state law. However, their existence should be known to every employee in the department. Simple, you say? I have handled situations when the employee and his chain of command were unaware of the existence of such an entity. Why? Well, no one ever appealed any discipline.

Do not expect your attorney to know all of these policies, procedures, ordinances, and other sources of rights. Give them a copy of your policy manual, because every government entity is different. You may be the first firefighter from that department to seek out this attorney. Also, remember the attorney will need time to get up to speed on the relevant policies. Don't wait until the day before the hearing to hire an attorney. Yes, this happens to me about three or four times every year.

State Law

Employee rights vary in the United States. Often, even neighboring states will have vastly different rules. Below are the two most typical arrangements[11] regarding the status of employees. However, this is another opportunity for you to consult with any attorney who handles these matters in your state to learn the meaning of each, or see if your state is a hybrid of the two. Knowing the laws in your state and your employee status is critical to understanding your rights.

> **At-Will Employment**: The employee has no right to continued employment. She can be fired for any or no reason. However, she cannot be fired for an unlawful reason. As you may have guessed, in this environment, it is often difficult to

prove that a person was fired for an unlawful reason. Under this model, absent a policy, ordinance, or other provision of the government or department, the employee will generally not have any rights if they are accused of misconduct or disciplined, including termination.

Right to Work[12]: The employee has a right to continued employment unless and until they violate a work rule or policy. Employees can still be let go without cause due to a layoff or a reduction in force. However, absent extenuating circumstances, an employer cannot institute any discipline without cause.

It is essential to know what model your state follows. You can learn this information through your state Department of Labor website, by examining your state constitution, or by checking with a local attorney who works in the employment arena. Your union may also have a pamphlet that explains your rights under state law and any collective bargaining agreement.

City Charters

City charters are a treasure chest of information. You can usually find them online at www.municode.com or on file at the city clerk's office. Counties have similar provisions. These are mini "constitutions" that set out the foundation of how the government entity operates. You may find entire sections on personnel, rights of employees, or small provisions that explain or establish the relationship between the government entity and employees. It is important to note that these documents typically control or take precedence if there is a conflict with the department or government policies. I have surprised more than one human resources director or chief with provisions of the city charter with which they were completely unfamiliar.

Collective Bargaining Agreements

Collective bargaining agreements (CBA) are contracts that specific units of employees sign with their employing agencies. They tend to be very specific, covering everything from pay, health benefits, employee rights, and other conditions of employment. Whenever a firefighter covered under a CBA contract is looking to determine the rights afforded them during an investigation or following the implementation of discipline, they should start with their CBA. As a member of the employee unit, you should automatically be covered by and have the protections of the CBA in place with the government. There is no need to sign on to the CBA, and you take the CBA as a whole. There is generally no way for you, as an individual, to change the terms.

Obviously, not all firefighters can look to a CBA for guidance. Your human resources department will know if there is a CBA in place for your agency and bargaining unit. Remember that membership in a union does not automatically mean a CBA is in place. I represent fire unions in the southern United States. Most do not have a CBA. This is a function of state law and custom. In other states, every department may have a CBA in place.

Employment Contracts

Any entity, public or private, can employ firefighters through an employment contract. A contract is nothing more than an agreement between parties that sets out the exact nature of the relationship, the obligations of the parties to each other and to others, the terms of the relationship with respect to pay and benefits, and how the relationship will be governed and ultimately ended. An employment contract is typically between an entity and one individual, as opposed to a CBA that covers groups of employees.

It is unusual for firefighters to be employed pursuant to an employment contract, because government employees tend to be employed in large numbers and the terms and conditions of their employment are more easily set out in policies and ordinances. Employment contracts are most often used with fire chiefs to offer protection from political whims, or applied to specific parts of the employment process. For example, a firefighter may be asked to sign a contract that requires reimbursement to their agency if they leave to go to another department within a specified time. This is typically done to obtain reimbursement for training. However, an employment contract may set out the firefighter's rights in the event of an investigation or appeal. The employment contract may also reference the policies, charter, or rules of the government entity.[13] However, if there is a conflict between the language of the contract and the policies, rules, or charter, the employment contract will likely control, unless it is found to be illegal or contrary to public policy.[14] This occurs because the contract is presumed to be a specific, private, and negotiated agreement, whereas the policies, rules, and charter are general without any "bargained for" exchange. In short, policies and procedures are mandates or guidelines put into place without any input from employees.

If there is an employment contract in play, make certain you have several copies available: one at home, one in your office, one stored on your laptop, one stored on your phone. You may not have access to your work computer, for example, if you are placed on administrative leave, so having several backups will come in handy. Make certain the copies are readable so you can reference them in a hurry to understand and assert any rights you may have. Most important, provide a copy to your attorney immediately upon consultation.

Due Process Clauses of State and Federal Constitutions

Due process in the United States provides a person two things: notice and an opportunity to be heard. Unless an employee is truly an "at-will" employee, as defined above, they are generally considered to have some type of due process rights. This is especially true if they can only be fired for cause. When this is the case, the employee is said to have a "property interest" in their job.[15] If an employee has a property interest in their job, they have a right to due process before that right can be taken away.

The practical application of at-will status is that an employee must be advised of the charges or policy violations against them, be provided an opportunity to respond to the charges or allegations, and be advised of the employment decision. In some instances, this process is set out in great detail in policy. In others, the process is left up to interpretation, allowing the supervisors and senior management to decide within the context of the policy what steps they must take to ensure the employee is provided due process. However, leaving this information up to interpretation can lead to due process violations if someone misses a step in the procedure or if the policies are not consistently applied.[16]

It is important to remember that every state has its own constitution with provisions that provide rights to citizens of that state.

It is important to remember that every state has its own constitution with provisions that provide rights to citizens of that state. While the state constitution can provide more rights to an employee, the federal constitution provides the "floor" and minimum rights.[17] However, the rights, the extent of those rights, and how you invoke those rights vary greatly based upon the department in which you work, the level of government for which you work, and often the state in which you work. So, you guessed it, contact an attorney in your area if you have any questions.

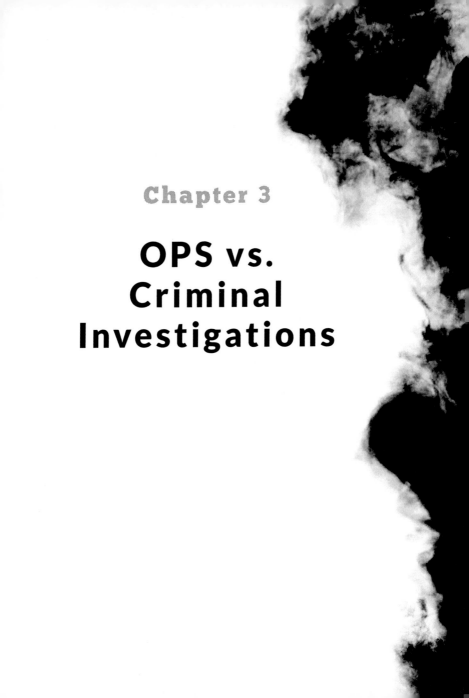

Chapter 3

OPS vs. Criminal Investigations

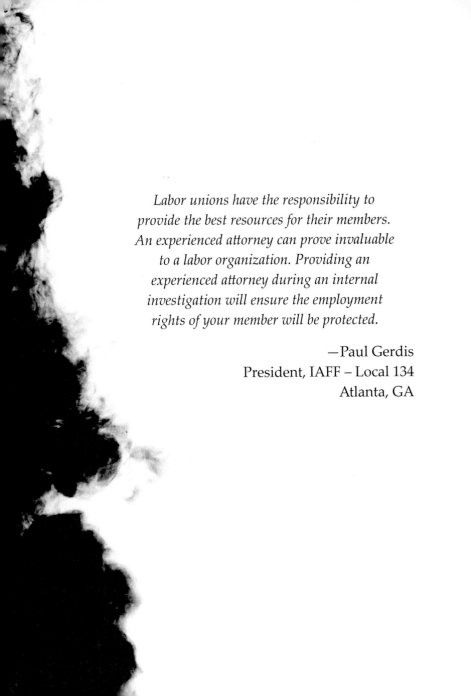

Labor unions have the responsibility to provide the best resources for their members. An experienced attorney can prove invaluable to a labor organization. Providing an experienced attorney during an internal investigation will ensure the employment rights of your member will be protected.

—Paul Gerdis
President, IAFF – Local 134
Atlanta, GA

If you are a firefighter, your conversations with other firefighters typically do not begin with these words: *"You have the right to remain silent."* However, every allegation of criminal misconduct will result in a criminal investigation by LEOs and an administrative investigation conducted by other firefighters. Aside from the stress of the criminal allegations, sitting in a room with one or two investigators, criminal or OPS, can be one of the worst experiences for a firefighter.

OPS investigations are administrative in nature and not criminal. They look into violations of policy, which include the obligation to conform to state and federal laws. So, for example, getting a DUI can automatically result in a violation of department or city policy. However, administrative investigations are also focused on identifying possible training deficiencies, determining whether policies should be modified or new policies should be created, evaluating equipment and procedures, considering whether employment and promotional selection procedures are appropriate and working, and regulating any other aspect of the department.

I teach OPS and IA investigators on a fairly regular basis. I have advice for them that I believe is helpful here for firefighters of all ranks and assignments. Every OPS investigation must

> OPS investigations are administrative in nature and not criminal.

begin with a premise and a focus on one basic, undeniable fact about the firefighter under investigation: you recruited, selected above other candidates, and trained this firefighter. At one time, a lot of people had faith and made extraordinary investments in her future. They may have made a mistake, they may have done something terrible, or they may have been falsely accused. In any event, they deserve your respect, if for no other reason than because they are a reflection of your recruiting, hiring, and training processes.

Criminal investigations, on the other hand, are focused on one thing: is there probable cause to believe a person violated a criminal statute? As such, the criminal investigation is more narrowly focused and often more time-sensitive. This is also the reason why criminal investigations are done by LEOs and not OPS investigators, even if the OPS investigators are also sworn as LEOs.

The most important thing for any firefighter to remember during the criminal investigation is the first few words of the Miranda warning: You have the *right* to remain silent. You are not required to speak with any criminal investigator about anything. If you choose not to speak with the criminal investigators, you cannot be disciplined or fired, and your silence cannot be used against you in any criminal proceeding.[18] This is your right under the United States Constitution, and likely under your state constitution[19] as well.

There are three critical decisions for every firefighter regarding a statement to criminal investigators:

1. Timing of your statement: I believe the first and most critical decision is the timing of the statement. You should NEVER give a statement to anyone, especially criminal investigators, if you are overwhelmed, tired, or not in control of your emotions.

2. Presence of counsel: The second decision is whether you will insist on having an attorney present. After all, as the Miranda warning further states, *"You have the right to have an attorney present during any questioning."* This is also a right guaranteed by the United States Constitution.

3. Your level of participation in the investigation: The entire process is voluntary. Therefore, you can decide how much you want to cooperate. You can choose to simply make a statement, answer questions, or put a time limit on the interview. These decisions begin with an understanding of a concept that bears repeating: statements to criminal investigators and participation in a criminal investigation are *voluntary*.

> *The most important thing for any firefighter to remember during the criminal investigation is the first few words of the Miranda warning: You have the right to remain silent.*

Statements to criminal investigators and partic- ipation in a criminal investiga- tion are voluntary. Many firefighters think they do not need an attorney if they do not believe they did anything wrong. Remember, this is only your perception. First and foremost, you may be incorrect. Second, it doesn't matter whether you believe you did nothing wrong. If the investigators believe they have evidence of criminal misconduct, they will have a mindset consistent with that belief. They are, after all, human beings. Third, if there is a case of mistaken identity or a false report of a crime, you will likely have only one opportunity to clear the matter up before the case proceeds further. You should consult with an attorney prior to making any statements to ensure you are prepared, are fully aware of the charges and the scope of the investigation, and can bring documents or other materials with you that may help establish your innocence.

 HOT TIP

I always recommend having an attorney involved as quickly as possible when you are made aware of any potential criminal charges, and that you meet with them prior to making any statements to any entity.

OPS and Criminal Investigations: Parallel Lines Do Not Cross[20]

Since the late 1960s, government employees have enjoyed specific protection during OPS investigations. Follow me as I walk you through the brief history, because it is important for you to know the background. In essence, because a public employer can force a public employee to answer questions during an investigation and crimes are prosecuted by the government, there are safeguards in place to ensure information and statements firefighters provide during OPS investigations cannot generally be used against them in a criminal case. As long as the firefighter tells the truth, with very few exceptions, what they say during an OPS investigation will not resurface in a criminal courtroom. Because of this, the law requires that OPS and criminal investigations remain separate. The public wins either way because the true purpose of OPS investigations is not only to determine policy violations, but also to examine the effectiveness of training, policies, and equipment.

In 1967, the United States Supreme Court (USSC) issued an opinion entitled *Garrity v. State of New Jersey*. The *Garrity* opinion, as you can imagine, has been studied and examined by courts and agencies all over the United States. Fortunately, the critical points in *Garrity* hold true today. These points are based on three simple principles:

Principle 1: An agency has an obligation and a right to investigate allegations of misconduct and incidents that involve its firefighters. These *administrative* investigations, typically conducted by OPS, are focused on clearing firefighters, determining the effectiveness of policies and training, and maintaining the integrity of the agency.

Principle 2: The agency should be able to compel firefighters to comply with OPS investigations. This principle is based upon the focus of OPS investigations as a means to evaluate policy, procedure, and equipment while determining if a firefighter was in compliance with agency policy.

Principle 3: A firefighter, like any other citizen, has the right to remain silent during any *criminal* investigation. As Justice Douglas stated in the *Garrity* opinion, "We conclude that policemen, like teachers and lawyers, are not relegated to a watered-down version of constitutional rights."[21]

You can see an actual *Garrity* warning used by an OPS unit in Appendix C. Familiarize yourself with it now so you are not forced to understand it while under stress.

In 2010, the Georgia Supreme Court issued an opinion entitled *State v. Thompson*.[22] Following a shooting, DeKalb County Police Officer Torrey Thompson gave statements both to internal affairs investigators and criminal investigators. Prior to the statements and two "walk-throughs" of the scene, supervisors told him he was not permitted to leave the area to avoid the media gathered at the scene. The Georgia Supreme Court held that Officer Thompson's "subjective belief" that he would be punished if he did not cooperate with the criminal investigators was sufficient for the court to find that his statements to the investigators were NOT voluntary. Therefore, the State could not use those statements against him in a criminal case charging him with murder. It is important to note that Officer Thompson told the court the agency's policy manual required him to participate in investigations, he was told he was not free to leave, he was *never explicitly told* that he had to cooperate and answer questions of the criminal investigators, and the criminal and internal affairs investigations were taking place *simultaneously*. Therefore, it was reasonable for him to believe he was required to answer any of the criminal investigators' questions.

The Georgia Supreme Court determined that the trial

court must examine the "totality of the circumstances" to decide if the officer had a *reasonable subjective* belief that he was forced to provide the statements at issue. Essentially, because the officer reasonably believed, based upon the totality of the circumstances, that he was required to answer the questions of the criminal investigators or risk discipline or job loss, those statements could not be used against him in a criminal trial because the investigation was a compelled, administrative investigation. Remember that the officer had a right not to speak with criminal investigators at all.

 HOT TIP

State v. Thompson *involved a LEO; however, the principles regarding OPS versus criminal investigations are the same. Even though this is a Georgia case, your attorney may be able to use it to help you in another state. It is important to consult an attorney licensed in your state to ensure your statements during administrative investigations are protected.*

So, a few questions to consider:

- Are you familiar with your agency's policies regarding investigations?
- Are you familiar with and able to articulate the

statutes and case law of your state regarding administrative investigations?

- Most important, do you still believe you should not have a lawyer present if you are accused of committing a criminal act? Are you willing to risk your livelihood and freedom just so you can do it yourself?

These are things to think about now—*before* you get a call from an investigator.

The Role of Counsel

Generally, a strict reading of *Garrity* does not allow for a right to counsel during an administrative investigation. However, I have spoken with and lectured to a lot of supervisors and management-level employees and encouraged them to allow employees to have attorneys present during administrative interviews. The practice increases transparency and protects OPS investigators and the agency from allegations of misconduct. Inclusion of attorneys may be required in a state with a firefighter bill of rights, in an agency that provides a right to counsel, or in an agency with a collective bargaining agreement in place under the *Weingarten* decision.[23] I have only been excluded from one administrative interview. I must say this was a silly decision for the law enforcement administrator who excluded me.

When you exclude counsel from an administrative interview, you provide him plenty of ammunition during the appeal process. You and your investigators will be forced to admit, under oath at an appeal hearing or in court, that your agency allows suspects to have counsel, but does not extend the same courtesy to employees.

The role of counsel at an administrative interview is the subject of some controversy. While courts have consistently permitted counsel to be present at any interview that involves the potential use of the information in a criminal case, the protections afforded under *Garrity* are a double-edged sword. In *Lingler v. Fechko*, an interesting opinion from the Sixth Circuit Federal Court of Appeals, the court held that the right to counsel and the right against self-incrimination *did not* extend to an interview that explicitly was not criminal in nature, even though the investigation had the potential to involve criminal activities.[24] You should assume you have no guaranteed right to counsel in an administrative interview absent a specific policy, state statute, or collective bargaining agreement that provides such rights. However, I urge you to make efforts to secure such rights in your agency. In addition, it never hurts to ask to have an attorney present. Contrary to what you may hear around the station, I do not agree with the people who say having an attorney with you makes you look guilty.

While the *Garrity* Court did not specifically spell out the right to have counsel present or the role of counsel at an administrative interview, the Court did say the following:

> We held in *Slochower v. Board of Education* that a public school teacher could not be discharged merely because he had invoked the Fifth Amendment privilege against self-incrimination when questioned by a congressional committee:
>
> "The privilege against self-incrimination would be reduced to a hollow mockery if its exercise could be taken as equivalent either to a confession of guilt or a conclusive presumption of perjury.... The privilege serves to protect the innocent who otherwise might be ensnared by ambiguous circumstances."
>
> We conclude that policemen, like teachers and lawyers, are not relegated to a watered-down version of constitutional rights.
>
> We now hold the protection of the individual under the Fourteenth Amendment against coerced statements prohibits

use in subsequent criminal proceedings of statements obtained under threat of removal from office, and that it extends to all, whether they are policemen or other members of our body politic.

It is difficult to read these sections of the *Garrity* opinion and conclude that firefighters should not be entitled to counsel during an administrative interview. This is especially true when the *Garrity* opinion followed on the heels of the *Miranda v. Arizona* decision that gave rise to the rights of the same name. However, this is the current state of the law. In a profession that begins with an oath to uphold the Constitution of the United States, it is appalling that some firefighters are not entitled to have an attorney present during administrative interviews. After sitting with many firefighters and speaking with many agency heads, I have yet to hear an intelligent argument for excluding attorneys at this stage of an investigation.

Keep in mind that *Garrity* was a plurality opinion, meaning the Court was divided with five justices voting for the opinion and four dissenting or disagreeing. Essentially, this means the case easily could have been decided against the rights of the firefighters. The bottom line is this: if you want the right to have counsel present during an administrative interview, push for changes in policies, the city charter, or county ordinances to guarantee that right. This may mean using the legislative process and political supporters to advocate on your behalf.

Garrity was not the last case to address this issue, and unfortunately, it will likely be examined by courts in the future. The USSC revisited this issue a year later in *Uniformed Sanitation Men Ass'n v. Comm'r of Sanitation of City of New York*, 392 U.S. 280 (1968). The Court again iterated that public employees are entitled to remain silent in the face of a *criminal* investigation. The Court went further, stating that unless the public employee was given clear immunity for statements, the employee could not be compelled to provide testimony, nor could the employee be terminated for failing to do so. The language of this case is clear and strong:

If you want the right to have counsel present during an administrative interview, push for changes in policies, the city charter, or county ordinances to guarantee that right.

> [The employees] were not discharged merely for refusal to account for their conduct as employees of the city. *They were dismissed for invoking and refusing to waive their constitutional right against self-incrimination. . . .*
>
> *They were entitled to remain silent because it was clear that New York was seeking not merely an accounting of their use or abuse*

of their public trust, but testimony from their own lips which, despite the constitutional prohibition, could be used to prosecute them criminally.

This case is often overlooked in firefighter circles because it does not involve firefighters. However, the case directly addresses the protections afforded public employees of any title. Consider this last quote:

> Petitioners as public employees are entitled, like all other persons, to the benefit of the Constitution, including the privilege against self-incrimination. [Citations omitted.] At the same time, petitioners, being public employees, subject themselves to dismissal if they refuse to account for their performance of their public trust, *after proper proceedings, which do not involve an attempt to coerce them to relinquish their constitutional rights.*

The issue of employee rights and the lines between OPS and criminal investigations has been explored many times by our courts. In 1973, the United States Court of Claims issued an opinion in the case of *Kalkines v. United States*, 473 F.2d 1391 (Ct. Cl. 1973) (amended on rehearing).[25] This case is quite instructive and has been cited many times by courts examining the rights of employees who are under investigation. The case is also an illustration of how administrative investigations can get off track, how investigators can lose focus, and how persistent firefighters and their attorneys must be to protect the firefighter's constitutional rights. Appendix D contains a sample Kalkines Warning so you can read an explanation of your rights in the language typically used during investigations.

Kalkines worked for the Bureau of Customs. In 1967, he was under investigation for impropriety based upon an allegation that he accepted $200 in exchange for favorable treatment on a customs entry. Kalkines was interviewed on four separate occasions in two states. At some point, he retained an attorney. Over the course of the investigation, he was made aware that criminal charges could arise from the acts alleged against him. He was also advised that these four interviews constituted an administrative investigation. However, Kalkines would not cooperate, because he was not provided immunity from prosecution for any statements he made during the administrative investigation or from any information gleaned from his statements. At the end of this process, the agency terminated Kalkines for failing to cooperate with an administrative investigation.[26] He appealed through his agency's appellate procedure and eventually to the United States Court of Claims.

It is important to note that the investigation at issue

took place while the *Garrity* and *Sanitation* cases were being briefed, argued, and decided by the USSC. In short, this was a new area of law. However, in the *Kalkines* opinion we see a clear statement by a federal court of the strength of the constitutional principles at issue.

The *Kalkines* Court reversed the termination of the employee, stating that the employee was clearly and justifiably concerned about a pending criminal investigation, and in that investigation, he had a constitutional right to remain silent. The Court placed the burden *on the agency* to show that Kalkines had clearly been told this was an administrative investigation *and* that he was entitled at all times to immunity for any statements made during that investigation. This was especially true when Kalkines expressed his concern about the nature of the investigation in light of the pending criminal case:

> The agent replied "that the following interview is administrative in nature, that it is not criminal, that there is no criminal action pending against you and that the purpose of this interview is entirely on an employer-employee basis and that furthermore any answers given to questions put to you in the interview cannot and will not be used against you in any criminal action. . . ."[27]

> But even the agent's most explicit

statement was incomplete since it did not refer to the fruits of the answers (in addition to the answers themselves). Moreover, and very significantly, the remainder of the colloquy shows that plaintiff was still very concerned about a criminal prosecution and that the agent never properly brought home that he would have immunity with respect to his answers.[28]

Even though the government claimed these warnings were sufficient, the Court disagreed.

The government in *Kalkines* also attempted to place the burden on the employee and his attorney to know immunity was attached to statements made during an administrative investigation. The Court rejected this position:

The Government suggests that Mr. Kalkines, or at least his lawyer, should have known that his answers (and their fruits) could not be used to his disadvantage, and therefore that the explicit caution mandated by *Uniformed Sanitation Men II* might be omitted. *With respect to the plaintiff, a frightened layman, this is certainly an unacceptable position; he could not be expected to know what lawyers and judges were even then arguing about. The case is hardly better for insisting that the attorney should have known, and should have been responsible for alerting his client.*[29]

The Court further expressed its displeasure with this argument stating as follows:

Plaintiff was not "duly advised of his options and the consequences of his choice." Quite the opposite, *he was left to squirm with a choice he should not have been put to—the possibility of going to jail or of losing his job.*[30]

There can be no doubt that the agency will bear the burden in this area at all times. The same is true in a criminal case, where the government must prove a confession was provided knowingly and voluntarily.[31]

As in every case, the *Kalkines* Court set forth its reasoning. The opinion sets out the factors that should be considered in this analysis:

The essential aspects are four: First, in describing a "conduct" investigation the *agent clearly indicated that a criminal investigation or trial was still possible*; he contented himself with reiterating that his own concern was "administrative" and he was not pursuing a violation of criminal law, without denying that a criminal proceeding could possibly eventuate. Second, the *agent never really responded to plaintiff's query as to whether the criminal investigation had been dropped, and did not tell him that the U.S. Attorney had refused to go forward with prosecution.* Third, the *agent failed to repeat or even refer to the earlier statement about non-use for criminal purposes of* [Kalkines'] *plaintiff's answers* in this "administrative" inquiry. Fourth, [Kalkines] *was obviously, and quite reasonably, left uncertain as to the connection between the questioning he was then being asked to undergo and a potential criminal action.* This last element seems to us reinforced by some confused remarks of [Kalkines] later on in the exchange—after the agent had commenced to ask specific questions—which seem to express great doubt about the separation between the civil and criminal sides of the investigation.[32]

It is interesting that thirty years prior to the decision in *State v. Thompson*, cited earlier, the Kalkines case analyzed the subjective beliefs of a government employee and the effect of the statements made by the investigators.

So, what was the outcome? Well, the case did not end well for the agency. The language is worth reading. Here is the exact quote:

> By failing to make and maintain a clear and unequivocal declaration of plaintiff's "use" immunity,[33] the customs agents gave the employee very good reason to be apprehensive that he could be walking into the criminal trap if he responded to potentially incriminating questions, and that in that dangerous situation he very much needed his lawyer's help. The record compels this conclusion. Perhaps the agents were not more positive in their statements because there still remained at that time the possibility of prosecution. Whatever the basis for their failure to clear up plaintiff's reasonable doubts, we are convinced the record shows that he was not "duly advised of his options and the consequences of his choice." His failure to respond was excused on this occasion, as on the earlier dates cited in the other specifications. The agency and the Civil Service Commission erred in disregarding this justification and in

holding that the duty to respond was
absolute and was violated.

> The *result is that, for this reason, plaintiff's
> discharge in 1968 was invalid, and he is now
> entitled to recover his lost pay, less offsets.*[34]

Kalkines is a great case to illustrate the risks to the
department if OPS investigators are not clear on the law
and their role in the investigation, and do not communicate well with the firefighters they investigate. This is
especially true in this last quote, which outlines the use
of and value of statements improperly solicited during
an administrative interview, as well as the authority of
an agency to terminate a firefighter who refuses to comply with an administrative investigation after properly
being advised of his rights.

> It is now settled that the individual cannot
> be discharged simply because he invokes
> his Fifth Amendment privilege against
> self-incrimination in refusing to respond.
> Conversely, a later prosecution cannot
> constitutionally use statements (or their
> fruits) coerced from the employee—in
> an earlier disciplinary investigation or
> proceeding—by a threat of removal from
> office if he fails to answer the question.
> But *a governmental employer is not wholly*

barred from insisting that relevant informa-
tion be given it; the public servant can be
removed for not replying if he is adequately
informed both that he is subject to discharge
for not answering and that his replies (and
their fruits) cannot be employed against him
in a criminal case.[35]

> *Here's the bottom line. OPS and criminal investigations are separate inquiries with different goals and must be kept separate. While you can be forced to answer questions during an OPS investigation, your answers cannot generally be used against you in a criminal case.*

This principle has been upheld and expanded. With the immunity from prosecution comes the requirement to cooperate or face termination.[36]

Here's the bottom line. OPS and criminal investigations are separate inquiries with different goals and *must* be kept separate. While you can be forced to answer questions during an OPS investigation, your answers cannot generally be used against you in a criminal case. The most notable exception to this rule is if you lie to the OPS investigators. In that case, you can be prosecuted for false statements, obstruction, or a similar charge. The concepts could not be more clear. An administrative investigation must be separate from a criminal investigation, and the employee is entitled to a clear and complete expression of immunity from criminal prosecution if he is compelled to testify with an administrative investigation. This means you must make certain you know whether you are speaking to an OPS investigator or a criminal investigator and should not be asked to speak with both at the same time.

FRONT-LINE STORY

A government employee is called into a conference room to speak about an incident that occurred on duty the week before. She recognizes two of the people in the room as OPS investigators. The other two are strangers. One of the OPS investigators begins the meeting by introducing the two strangers as LEOs from a city within the county firefighter's jurisdiction. The OPS investigator advises that the LEOs have a few questions for her. The firefighter, through her attorney, advises that she will cooperate fully with any OPS investigation, but will make a separate decision whether to speak with the LEOs, and the LEOs cannot be present during the OPS inquiry.

Hopefully you've realized there's more to an investigation than showing up as ordered and hoping for the best. It is critical to know who is asking the questions and what is being investigated. Like any right, you can waive the protections afforded to you under the law, a constitution, or a policy. But be prepared for the fact that you may become the subject of, or at least a witness to, an official investigation. Learn your rights ahead of time, and have a plan in place to protect those rights.

Chapter 4

What to Expect While Under Investigation

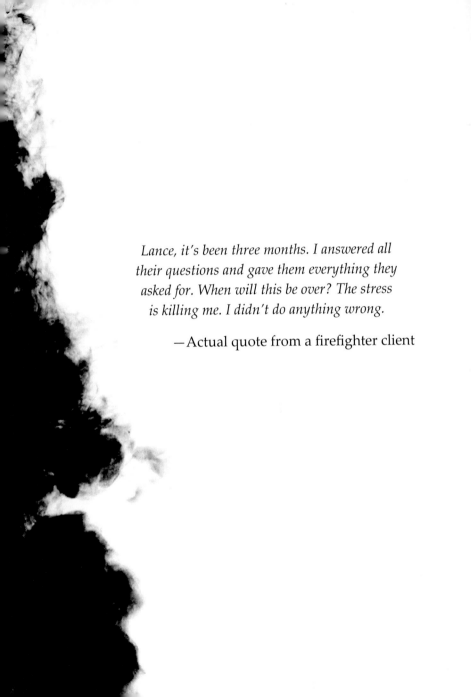

Lance, it's been three months. I answered all their questions and gave them everything they asked for. When will this be over? The stress is killing me. I didn't do anything wrong.

—Actual quote from a firefighter client

What happens when you receive a letter, an email, or worse, an oral warning from a supervisor advising that you are under investigation? Like most of my clients, many thoughts may go through your mind: *What is this about? Am I just a witness, or did someone file a complaint? Did I do something wrong? Will this end in a write-up, a butt-chewing, days off, or a termination?*

Unfortunately, many firefighters are not told the nature of the investigation, the allegations against them, or even when the supposed infractions occurred. This is often the case even when the policy of the department specifically requires this information be provided *before* the interview with OPS. How can anyone prepare to give a statement without advanced knowledge of the allegations? A fair, focused, and professional investigation benefits from having a firefighter who has read the relevant incident reports, reviewed the appropriate policies, and taken the time to think about the events that may have occurred months ago.

 FRONT-LINE STORY

Several years ago, I represented a paramedic working for a very busy EMS and fire service who was called into OPS without notice to answer questions about a call that occurred eighteen months prior. Unfortunately, he did not consult an attorney prior

to participating in the administrative interview and investigation. He was not permitted to review any reports or the available video that captured all of the relevant events, even though his department's policy required advanced notice of both the interview and the nature of the allegations against him. He was terminated when his recollection of the events, not unexpectedly, differed from the video. He ran hundreds of calls between the call at issue in the investigation and the day of his interview. He was then saddled with the burden of being labeled as having been untruthful during an internal investigation. As a result, he also faced sanctions through the state against his paramedic license. When we last spoke, he was pursuing a degree to enter another profession. He was disgusted with the treatment he had received and had difficulty obtaining any employment due to the comments and conclusions contained in his personnel and OPS files. The jurisdiction and taxpayers lost thousands of dollars in training due to poor investigation procedures. Fortunately, we were able to extricate him from the civil suit that resulted and was fueled in large part by the shoddy investigation and conclusions of his agency.

Unless they are aware of the exact circumstances that gave rise to the complaint, because it occurred recently or the firefighter expected an investigation or complaint, many firefighters do not consider seeking legal counsel when they are first notified of an investigation. They adopt a reasonable position of "I don't need a lawyer yet. I will just see what this is about." Understandably, they trust their agency and the process. All too often, however, they find themselves knee-deep in a controversy and ill prepared to respond to questions or produce documents and information that will explain their actions, prove their actions were appropriate, or exonerate themselves.

I have found that in most cases, when severe discipline is expected for any reason, firefighters often scramble to seek legal counsel and assistance preparing for the OPS interview and process. This is often done under extreme time pressure.

You go through the interview, and it is pretty intimidating. Although you expected a calm, professional question-and-answer session, you find yourself in an adversarial encounter during which you are asked direct, detailed questions that you are expected to answer quickly. You find that your statements indicating you do not recall specific conversations or dates only serve to frustrate the investigator and lead to allegations that you may be concealing the truth or failing to cooperate. You are aware that both conclusions in a report could result in your termination. The investigator presents documents, photographs, and policies, and demands that you explain your actions. When the interview is done, you find yourself trying to sort out what just happened and drive home still trying to remember the details of the conversations and calls that occurred weeks, months, or even a year ago.

As you leave the interview, you may feel like you answered everything to the best of your ability. You think to yourself, *I don't need a lawyer yet. I will see if they clear me.* Sometime later, you receive a notice to appear before the head of your agency to discuss the results and findings of the investigation. Some firefighters still think, *I don't need a lawyer yet. I'll see what the chief has to say.* The chief meets with you, advises the charges were sustained, and says you have an opportunity to state your case one last time. At this point, most firefighters think, *I wish I had a lawyer. How did this happen?!*

So, you hire a lawyer to appeal the chief's decision. The lawyer will now file the appeal based on the letter you received, the interview you gave, and the meeting you had with the chief. For better or worse, your attorney can only work with the case you hand him. In addition, it may be difficult to present statements or documents that assist your case at this point, as the chain of command, and the investigators, have come to their conclusions at the end of what they believe is a complete investigation.

The role of a lawyer in an internal investigation is

complicated. As discussed earlier, your rights during such investigations may arise from a provision of your city charter, county ordinances, your state constitution, the United States Constitution, a collective bargaining agreement, or the policies of your agency. Even though the role of an attorney may be limited in many instances, the role of the attorney as a counselor is *never* limited. An attorney can help you ensure your rights are protected, make certain you review the appropriate policies and documents prior to making any statements, and help you organize your thoughts. This includes being prepared to supply the investigators with a list of witnesses and documents that assist your case or clarify the facts of the investigation.

When you do not involve an attorney until the appeal phase, your attorney is forced to appeal the "record" you hand him. Any missteps, gaps in your memory, or misstatements will likely affect the strength of your appeal. In some instances, a mistake on your part could preclude an appeal *entirely*. Administrative deadlines are *hard deadlines*. Missing a deadline may affect your rights. For example, if you fail to file for an appeal, you may lose not only the right to that level of appeal, but your right to appeal the decision in court.[37]

An attorney can help you ensure your rights are protected, make certain you review the appropriate policies and documents prior to making any statements, and help you organize your thoughts.

You should begin protecting your appeal rights as soon as you believe you may be subject to discipline.

HOT TIP

Develop a relationship with an attorney early to make it easier to reach out to him. When it comes to consulting an attorney early, an ounce of prevention is worth a pound of cure. You should not be searching the internet for an attorney after you receive notice that you are the subject of an OPS investigation.

Confidentiality

More often than not, when a firefighter is "under investigation," the entire agency knows about it. Let's face it, as public safety professionals we are good at respecting the public's right to privacy, but "scoop" on our coworkers is generally fair game. Those casual conversations and the ever-churning rumor mill present in many, if not most, agencies create a pitfall for firefighters.

Investigations into misconduct should be conducted in a confidential manner for several reasons. First and foremost, firefighters are professionals. An investigation into misconduct of a fellow professional is a serious matter. Therefore, the details, as well as the existence, of an investigation should be closely guarded to the same degree as a sensitive criminal investigation.

The second reason to keep these matters confidential is simple: until proven, an allegation is just that and nothing more. Agency administrators are highly conscious of keeping criminal allegations under wraps until investigators possess sufficient probable cause to bring charges against a citizen. The same respect and presumption of innocence must be afforded to firefighters who are under investigation. Sounds like a due process issue to me, but what do I know? I'm just a lawyer!

The third reason to avoid casual conversations about pending investigations is to protect the integrity of the process. Standard investigative techniques mandate that we separate witnesses to avoid tainting their impressions and potential testimony. When the agency is buzzing with rumors and innuendo about an administrative investigation, you risk tainting the information to be gleaned from interviews. Those tainted statements will surface again in personnel hearings, criminal cases, and lawsuits. By then, it is too late to "unring the bell." There is also a risk that someone in the chain of command will base their discipline on what they heard instead of the facts discovered during the investigation.

FRONT-LINE STORY

Just as a false criminal allegation can destroy the reputation of a private citizen, the mere allegation of misconduct, even if unfounded, can signal the end of a firefighter's career. We have represented more than one firefighter who was accused of dishonesty or sexual harassment. In each case, the investigations understandably took a great deal of time, involved many interviews by OPS investigators, and regrettably were not kept under wraps. Even though the firefighters were ultimately cleared of the allegations, a few had to change stations and one left the agency. Unfortunately, the rumor mill, as expected, failed to provide all the facts. The cloud of suspicion overshadowed the facts and the conclusions.

Finally, firefighters who are under investigation should beware of casual conversations with anyone. Remember that *Garrity* protections[38] apply to statements *compelled by management*. Any statements you make to a deputy chief who asks you what happened "off the record" may not be protected under *Garrity* unless you document the encounter and take steps to ensure such protection applies. If this occurs, you will be required to show a court that you subjectively believed you were required to answer those questions. I would hope such "off-the-record" conversations are not an attempt to entrap you, but I was not born yesterday. This is particularly important in any investigation involving an arrest, allegations of theft, or conduct which could form the basis of criminal charges in the future.[39]

HOT TIP

Here is my advice for administrators: Your agency should have a strict policy to keep any allegation of misconduct confidential. This includes investigations conducted by a criminal division, internal affairs, or at the supervisor level. The consequences for failing to keep such allegations confidential should be the same as the consequences for leaking information on a sensitive criminal investigation or sensitive HIPAA-protected information to the public.

For firefighters under investigation, speak only to the investigators and your attorney. Nothing good will come from discussing these matters with your coworkers. At minimum, you may taint the very testimony that could exonerate you. In the worst-case scenario, you may place a friend at the center of an investigation that does not concern her. If you are approached by anyone who desires to speak "off the record," you should respectfully decline the opportunity irrespective of the person's rank. You can rely upon the admonition from the OPS investigators that you not speak with anyone about the case. If this does not work, you can tell them you are under orders from your attorney not to discuss the matter without counsel present. Any lawyer will likely give you this instruction once engaged to represent you. If you do not have an attorney to assist with your defense, perhaps you should reconsider your decision to "go it alone."

For the rest of the firefighters in the agency, preserve and exemplify the highest standards of your profession by respecting the investigative process. Refuse to engage in the idle banter and rumor sharing, and discourage others from doing so. Remember that your "off-the-record" statement could change the direction of the investigation and become the pivotal piece of evidence in a disciplinary hearing or trial. How will you defend the fact that your statement was based upon a rumor? Most important, recognize that you could be under investigation tomorrow. What level of professionalism would you expect from your fellow professionals if you were the subject of the investigation?

FRONT-LINE STORY

Several years ago, I represented a LEO who was ultimately cleared of the underlying administrative charges against her. However, following the initial

OPS interview, she was called in, as were several coworkers, because a coworker heard her make a comment about the OPS interview. The OPS captain was concerned she and her coworkers had violated the order not to discuss the case. It was an uncomfortable situation for everyone involved, and nearly ended the career of one of the LEOs.

Isolation

The main complaint from firefighters who are under investigation is that they feel isolated. This is especially true if you are placed on leave while the investigation is ongoing. Even if you are not on leave, if everyone at your station is under strict orders not to discuss the facts of the case, you may find yourself in uncomfortable situations surrounded by coworkers who are all reluctant to speak about anything for fear of being disciplined. This is the main reason why I advocate for quick investigations and a fast track to providing the results to the affected employee. Often this goal is legitimately frustrated by OPS units that are short-staffed and investigators who do not work hours consistent with the rest of the department. Because the investigators only work during the day, the scheduling of interviews alone may take weeks or months.

HOT TIP

I want to provide some simple advice for firefighters who are under investigation and those who are not: talk to each other. Yes, you should absolutely avoid any discussion of the facts of a pending investigation. You should also avoid gossip or rumors about the investigation. However, you should work out with your buddies, go to the backyard barbeque celebrating the graduation of your shiftmate's child, and attend a ball game with your usual group of friends. You need, and should rely upon, that support network every day, more so when you are under stress at work.

The opportunity to speak with your friends, socialize with your coworkers, and support each other is essential to your well-being. You understand each other and share a bond of common experiences. While the investigation may be stressful enough, other factors may increase that anxiety, such as money problems if the firefighter is unable to work extra shifts or part-time jobs while the investigation is pending, media attention to the issues that gave rise to the investigation, or marital difficulties unrelated to the investigation. Do not let anyone stand alone during an investigation.

Preparation for an
OPS Investigation

Before you are ever notified of an investigation, you should read all the sections regarding OPS investigations in your policy manual from your department and your government employer. In fact, you should read these documents as soon as you finish this chapter!

In most cases, an investigation is conducted by OPS investigators. However, we are increasingly experiencing investigations conducted by human resources (HR) staff members. Typically, such investigations relate to discrimination, harassment, and allegations of unfair treatment and harassment. In our experience, investigations performed by HR personnel are problematic. Although they may have some training in how to interview employees, many we have encountered do not. They do not press for details or appropriately explore inconsistencies in statements between people interviewed. In the worst scenarios, we have read transcripts of interviews conducted by HR personnel who had difficulty forming clear and concise questions. This led to a disconnect between the subject of the questions and the intent and content of the answers. It is easy to see how these situations could lead to inaccurate conclusions and unfounded discipline.

The first step to prepare for any OPS investigation is to obtain a clear understanding of the allegations against you. Are you the main target? Is this misconduct in the form of a policy violation or an allegation of criminal wrongdoing? Does the OPS investigation relate to on-duty or off-duty conduct?

Second, determine what information you will need to properly prepare for the OPS interview. You will be required to provide truthful and complete answers. In order to do so, you may need to review documents, video and audio recordings, reports, calendars, shift rosters, run reports, call logs, and radio logs, as well as policies and procedures. This is especially true if the events occurred sometime before, or if the incident is the type encountered on a regular basis. In the latter case, it is easy for the facts of several incidents to "run together," and absent a significant event that made a particular call memorable, you may not have any specific recollection whatsoever that you can share with OPS. Remember that the incident is clearly memorable to the complainant, who may be able to recall specifics that meant nothing to you at the time and are therefore difficult or impossible for you to recount.

One of the most critical documents that can help you prepare for interviews is the calendar on your smartphone. Six months from today, will you recall if you worked A, B, or C shift? This may very well cause confusion during the OPS interview. You may work with a completely different set of people on different shifts. If the OPS investigation involves, for example, who was on a piece of apparatus with you on a call, knowing your shift may be the difference between being prepared with a clear answer and appearing uncooperative.

Remember that the law allows a person to provide testimony from their memory, their memory refreshed by a source of information such as a video, or directly from a "business" record such as an incident report even if they do not recall the events documented in the report.[40] It is expected, even under oath in front of a jury, that people may not have any specific recollection of events but can still offer important facts. Your OPS investigators must understand this.

Next, it is critical that you take time to review the information well in advance of the interview. It is not appropriate to review all of this material the day or night before, or worse, an hour before. The review of these materials may stimulate memories that will require time to sort out. You may also recall other materials related to this incident that may better prepare you for the OPS interview. Finally, you need time to digest the information you review. Remember, you are not seeking to get an overview. Your goal is to be prepared to relate details such as the date and time, addresses, the names and roles of coworkers, and the location of individuals during stressful events.

Although the actual investigation may not be available until the matter is closed, many "source" documents or information you can use to defend yourself should be available while the investigation is pending. Source documents may include Computer-Aided Dispatch (CAD) reports, phone records, policies, memos, training records, or schedules. Make certain your attorney obtains these items to allow you to prepare, if time permits. Further, make certain you review your own social media pages and those of your coworkers. Often, the focus of the investigation or the facts that surround the OPS inquiry can be found on social media.

Finally, you will need time to prepare for the interview with your legal representative. Make certain your attorney has all of the documents and materials you needed to prepare so they can become familiar with them. You should ensure you have thoroughly reviewed the documents before meeting with your attorney. The meeting with your attorney should also take place at least a day prior to the OPS interview. Appendix B includes a checklist for how to prepare for an OPS interview.

Commonly Asked Questions about OPS Interviews

We speak with a lot of public safety employees in our office. I thought it would be helpful to include some of the typical questions we receive.

Can I have an attorney present during my OPS interview?

This is an interesting question that depends on many factors. *Garrity v. New Jersey*[41] does not specifically state that a public employee is entitled to have an attorney present during OPS interviews. However, as stated in the previous chapter, the case does contain the following quote: "Police officers, like firefighters and teachers, are not entitled to a watered-down version of their constitutional rights." Justice Douglas was not clear about whether this statement applied to the underlying constitutional principles upon which the case was decided, namely the Fifth Amendment right against self-incrimination, or the right to counsel, which was not a central issue in the *Garrity* case.

As you can imagine, this issue has been litigated many times. Many federal courts have held that an employee does not have a right to counsel during an administrative interview.[42] In addition, even when a right to counsel has been found or included in policy, there seems to be a consensus that the role of the attorney is limited.[43] In a criminal case, the suspect or person interviewed has a right under the Sixth Amendment to have counsel present. That attorney can also have an active role in the interview, including asking questions, clarifying questions, having the client clarify her answers, conferring with the client, and most important, terminating the interview at any time. The law is clear that neither an attorney nor an employee can terminate an OPS interview without consequences, including termination.[44] This is the essence of the *Garrity* decision: an employee can be compelled to answer questions during an administrative interview and face discipline including, but not limited to, termination if they fail to do so or terminate the interview. Therefore, it is essential that the attorney you hire understands the limitations placed on him during the OPS investigative process.

FRONT-LINE STORY

Several years ago, I was involved in a case before a civil service board. I developed a good, professional relationship with the attorney for the board. He told me about an interesting issue that arose a few months prior. A department was interviewing a firefighter who had hired an attorney who mainly worked on criminal cases as a defense attorney and was not familiar with Garrity. *During the OPS interview, the attorney instructed his client not to answer a question. The OPS investigator properly told the attorney and the firefighter that he was required to answer the questions. The attorney continued to instruct his client not to answer. After several opportunities to come to a resolution, the OPS investigator finished the interview and once again asked the firefighter to answer the questions he had previously refused to answer. The attorney again instructed the firefighter not to answer. The OPS investigator wrote up his report. The department terminated the firefighter because he had refused to answer the OPS investigator's questions.*

The right to counsel varies with collective bargaining agreements (CBA). The union can negotiate the ability of the firefighter to have an attorney present during all questioning as part of the agreement.[45] In addition, the role of the attorney can also be set out in the CBA.

Some policies and procedures set out the exact role of attorneys in the disciplinary process. In my experience, very few specifically set out that firefighters are not entitled to have counsel present. Some set out that the attorney may be present, but cannot participate. Others set out that the client may have an attorney present and consult with the attorney as needed. Others still set out a hybrid of these positions.

Can I have a representative with me during the OPS interview?

This is also an open question, and it varies greatly across the United States. Typically, a person is permitted to have a representative present if there is a CBA in place. Absent a CBA, some departments will allow a representative to be present as a matter of policy (see Appendix E for a Sample Weingarten Rights Form). As with an attorney, the role of that representative varies.

If I have a choice, should I have a union representative or an attorney?

Okay, disclaimer time. I am an attorney who advocates zealously for my firefighter clients. Therefore, I always prefer that a firefighter have an attorney present during the OPS process, especially the interview. However, I also recognize that the firefighter, as well as the union or employee organization, may have difficulty paying for an attorney to attend every interview. Therefore, you must make a choice.

I believe there are times when a tactical decision must be made that affects the firefighter's appeal rights, as well as the disciplinary process. While I believe an attorney can assist in these situations, I have seen many capable union representatives and officers who do a great job for their members. As an attorney advising several fire unions, I make every effort to educate and coach the union representatives to increase their skills. I have also made myself available by phone during interviews in case the union representative had questions.

Here's the bottom line: if at all possible, under the rules, policies, statutes, or case law of where you live, have a person with you who can help you prepare for and navigate through the difficulties and challenges of an OPS investigation.

Answering Difficult Questions

You will face tough questions during an OPS interview. Expect them. Prepare for them. Do not get angry or defensive when you hear them. When you hear one, think about your answer and answer it.

Questions in an OPS interview may be difficult for four main reasons. First, you are nervous due to the process and the location of the interview. People do not think as well under stress as they do when relaxed. I personally believe, and I tell OPS investigators this when I speak to those groups, that the most effective OPS investigators are the ones who are calm and keep the firefighter relaxed. Second, the topic of conversation

The most effective OPS investigators are the ones who are calm and keep the firefighter relaxed.

may be extremely uncomfortable. I've represented many firefighters who were falsely accused of serious misconduct. Third, sometimes the environment is not ideal. I have heard telephones ringing and people talking, elevators working, HVAC systems kicking on and off, and numerous other unnecessary and frankly inappropriate distractions during OPS interviews. All this means you may not hear a question, you may need to ask someone to repeat part of their question, or they may not hear your answer. Finally, although you and the OPS investigator may be intelligent, well-spoken individuals who have a common base of knowledge and are fluent in the English language, spoken words are confusing at times. Be certain you understand their questions and they understand your answers.

Here is a list of questions that may cause you difficulty:

1. Questions that call for details regarding conversations.
2. Questions that call for details of events that occurred a long time ago.
3. Questions that call for details of events that occurred when you were under extreme stress, such as the scene of a fire, a prolonged rescue or

extrication, or any call when someone—or you—was injured.[46]

4. Questions that relate to something you wrote on a report, memo, social media post, or other document.

5. Questions regarding what other firefighters know, because you truly cannot say what they heard, saw, felt, smelled, or remember.

6. Questions regarding matters about which you have no information to offer.

7. Questions that require you to think before you answer.

8. Any question that requires you to draw a diagram.

9. Questions that push your memory because you were fatigued, taking medication, drinking, or otherwise distracted when the events occurred. The accurate and truthful answer may be that you cannot recall or do not remember. This can be uncomfortable.

10. Any question that is asked repeatedly or in different ways.

The important thing is to be honest, be consistent, be firm, and pause before you answer. Do not hesitate to tell the OPS investigator that her question relates to something that happened a long time ago, and you need to think before you answer. You should also be prepared to state that you need to look at documents or video in order to give a complete and accurate answer. Do not allow someone to force you to answer without the aid of an existing document that will allow you to give an accurate, complete answer.

Sometimes I believe the most difficult question asked during an OPS interview is this: Is there anything else? There may be times when you are able to provide all the information needed during the first OPS interview. This is, of course, more likely when you are aware of the charges and facts in advance and are permitted to prepare for the interview. If you have any concerns that you may think of additional information after the conclusion of the OPS interview, tell the OPS investigator you want to continue thinking about the questions and will follow up with any additional information.

There is no such thing as an "unofficial" conversation with anyone in OPS. Even if they are trying to help you, be polite, be professional, and listen more than you speak. Notify your attorney immediately if anyone from OPS contacts you directly once the department is aware you have representation.

Chapter 5

The Appeal Process

Any fool can make a rule,
and any fool will mind it.

—Henry David Thoreau

At least once every year, we have a firefighter or LEO in our office who looks a bit puzzled when we tell them we need to find out how appeals are conducted in their agency, the deadlines for the appeal process, and what rights they have. The truth is, the rules vary a great deal, and sometimes, there are no rules.

 FRONT-LINE STORY

Recently, I handled a case where the entire appeals process consisted of one paragraph—that is, until we approached the actual hearing date. Then, after over a month of sending open record requests for any and all rules, we received an email with thirteen detailed bullet points about how the appeal would proceed. How could this happen? The short answer is my client was the first to appeal that anyone in the city could remember.

We handle appeals all over the state of Georgia.[47] Appeals are typically governed by guidelines that may be found in policies, ordinances, city charters, collective bargaining agreements, or state administrative procedure acts.[48] In short, every jurisdiction has a different set of rules. What's more challenging is that many of those rules conflict, and some trump others. For example, we have found ourselves challenging the constitutionality of a small city ordinance. Even though the ordinance was properly passed and signed by the city council, it still may violate your state or federal constitutional rights.

As we stated in Chapter 3 on OPS investigations, you should take the time as soon as possible to learn these procedures and gather a copy of the relevant policies or CBA. Your attorney should discuss these issues with you when you first meet about your OPS investigation. You may think this is strange, but diligent attorneys always prepare for the stage of the litigation facing them and the appeal at the next stage. Many times, certain precautions must be taken at the outset to preserve your right to appeal later should you desire. For example, we typically pay for a court reporter to attend and record the testimony and proceedings at every appeal hearing. Although the agencies usually record the proceedings, tapes can break, recordings can be corrupted while saving them, and digital recorders can fail. Without an accurate transcript, it may be impossible to appeal or you may lose important testimony that can help at the next level of appeal.

The appeal process is more interactive than you may expect. Although this process is more "attorney driven" than the OPS interview, your attorney will need your input into strategy, the resources you are willing to expend, the names and locations of witnesses, your time to prepare your testimony, and sometimes something as simple as your signature. Therefore, be certain you stay in contact with your attorney and the staff of the law firm during this process. Keep in mind that you should never use your government cell phone or email to communicate with your attorney.

Many times, you do not have a choice to be involved in the appeal process. We have handled many cases in which the government entity made the decision to appeal after we won the case at the first level of appeal. Although this may result in increased attorney fees and expenses for you, your victory may be short-lived if you do not respond to the department's appeal.

Why Do Appeals Cost So Much?

Administrative appeals are a unique type of litigation. In fact, some attorneys do not handle them at all. We handle the entire case from the OPS interview through any appeals, some of which end up in trial and appellate courts. Appeals are unique because they typically fall into three categories:

1. A live, in-person hearing before an individual or board
2. An appeal to an individual or board based upon the submission of written documents only

3. Appeals filed in a court system that may involve hearings, but rely upon the submission of written documents, and perhaps the oral argument of the attorneys before a judge or a panel of judges

In each case, the time spent by the attorney will mount up quickly. In addition, the costs of court reporters, certified transcripts, travel, subpoenas, process servers, and even couriers can be high. A one-day hearing transcript can cost $2,000, subpoenas typically require a witness fee, and couriers often have minimum charges. Process server fees can increase considerably if people evade service, and I have experienced this in several cases.

Pre and Post Disciplinary Meetings

Many policies, CBAs, and other sources provide a firefighter with a chance to "add relevant information" prior to the final imposition of discipline. In addition, after the discipline is imposed, many times there is another opportunity for the firefighter to speak directly to the decision maker. Appendix F contains an example of a Notice of Proposed Discipline to demonstrate the wording typically used. These procedures vary, but they are based in sound management principles. In many cases, they are also based upon United States Supreme Court precedent.

The names of these procedures also vary. I have heard them called "name-clearing sessions," "pre–adverse action hearings," "post–adverse action hearings," "Kelly hearings," and "Loudermill hearings." I will spare you from the amusing nicknames these hearings sometimes are given within particular agencies. Irrespective of the name assigned to it, the purpose is to make certain the decision maker has all the information necessary to make an informed decision. However, there is another reason.

I teach law enforcement and fire management and command staff members on a regular basis.[49] When I teach classes on employment law, I encourage every agency to conduct these hearings even if they are not required to do so under the law or other procedure. The reason for this advice is that agencies are made up of people, and people make mistakes. OPS investigators can miss something. Supervisors can show favoritism, or the opposite, toward some employees. Employees can be mistaken or have poor recollections of events. Finally, some people can manipulate the disciplinary process to further their own agendas. These hearings are the last chance for the decision maker to avoid placing the agency at risk of facing a lawsuit or imposing discipline in an unfair or unlawful manner.

Agencies are made up of people, and people make mistakes.

FRONT-LINE STORY

I represented a LEO who was facing termination. The agency prepared a document that set out his disciplinary history. The document reflected that the LEO was placed on probation three times during his employment for periods of six months. The agency served the document on the LEO as required by the policy. When I reviewed it with the client, he was very frustrated. So was I. The agency did not have a "probation" period in their discipline policy, and neither did the city. We[50] raised this with the chief during the pre–adverse action hearing. This revelation caused a great deal of embarrassment for the command staff at the conference table, but my client was not terminated.

In addition, the decision maker should encourage the firefighter to speak at these stages of the disciplinary process. After all, I believe a fire chief would rather find out at this stage that an employee was threatened not to reveal information to the OPS investigators, or that the reason a female employee is chronically late is because she is avoiding the male supervisor who is demanding sex from her in exchange for preferential shifts. Like I said, fire departments are comprised of people, and people do strange things.

Witnesses, Subpoenas, Documents, and Testimony

Your attorney will need input from you to prepare for any hearings or meetings. I have handled a lot of appeals, but I have not worked in your specific agency. You need to provide your attorney with the specifics of how paperwork is routed, where documents are kept and maintained in the normal course of business, and other information.

Determining who to call as a witness, how to contact those people, and when they can be served with a subpoena to appear at the hearing are critical decisions and information that require your input.

If you will be speaking or testifying at a hearing, the attorney will need to meet with you to discuss the documents that will be entered into evidence, the questions he will ask, and the questions he anticipates the department will ask you on cross-examination. It is important that you prepare in advance of these meetings and work hard to help the attorney present your side of the case in a coherent and factual manner to persuade the board or decision maker.

> You need to provide your attorney with the specifics of how paperwork is routed, where documents are kept and maintained in the normal course of business, and other information.

Managing Appeal Procedures and Deadlines

At some point, the decision maker will make the discipline final. Appendix G contains a sample Discipline Notice with Appeal Options. This is typically the point at which all deadlines begin. They vary greatly between departments, and even as to the different stages of appeals. We have handled appeals with two-week deadlines and others with three-day deadlines. Some make allowances for weekends and holidays with deadlines stated in terms of "business days," and emergencies when offices are closed for other reasons. Others do not and strictly rely upon the calendar. We have handled cases that required service of the appeal by mail, fax, email, certified mail, in-person delivery, and formal service upon a specific individual. While this can be frustrating, the procedures are usually set out in a document, even though it may difficult to locate that information. The important thing is that if you miss a deadline, or fail to timely serve your notice of appeal or other documents in the proper manner, you may lose *all* your appeal rights.

The important thing is that if you miss a deadline, or fail to timely serve your notice of appeal or other documents in the proper manner, you may lose all your appeal rights.

HOT TIP

You should calendar every deadline on your personal calendar. You must keep in contact with your attorney and the law firm staff assigned to your case to check on these deadlines. You are well within your rights as a client to request copies of any filings and to be notified when appeals are filed. Appendix H contains a sample Appeal Notice.

Waiting for Decisions

This can be an extremely frustrating part of the process for our clients. All procedures and entities vary, but we have handled appeals that require the board or individual making the decision to issue their opinion within as few as five business days. Others have no time limit. In one extreme case, the civil service board that hears appeals was in such a state of flux that firefighters and other city employees had waited months for appeals to be heard.[51] We secured hearings only after threatening to file suit against the government entity.

If the department misses a deadline, the employee may be able to automatically proceed to the next level of appeal or force a reversal of the discipline. However, sometimes we are forced to wait because the language of the appeal decision may be critical. This is a sensitive area that requires strategic analysis to maximize the firefighter's opportunities for a favorable or acceptable outcome.

One question we often address is when the appeal is "final" according to the department. This can be critical when a firefighter is on a promotion list or waiting to take a promotion exam. This also becomes important if the firefighter is in the hiring process for another agency. Finally, this is also important if the state licensing agency[52] is conducting an investigation or considering action against the firefighter's certificates.

One procedure that also varies is whether the firefighter serves a suspension prior to appealing the matter. One local jurisdiction requires that the discipline be "served"—for example, the employee to lose the pay from a suspension—before their appeal rights arise. In other cases, the discipline is "withheld" until all appeals are final. The term "final" may mean many steps of appeals and delays of several months, or in extreme cases, for years.

The important thing to take away from this is that you must be patient. If you are working as the appeal progresses, make a conscious effort to be a model employee. Do not allow anyone to complain to the chief or your chain of command that you are causing a morale problem. Do not place yourself in a tight spot by being written up for policy violations during this time. Rest assured your chain of command will be watching you. If you are on administrative leave during this period, you must keep yourself occupied and follow all agency rules.

If you are on administrative leave without pay, you will need to bring income to your home. Your attorney can assist you in determining what types of work you can seek to avoid any problems with your agency during this stressful time.

To Appeal or Not to Appeal? It's Not an Easy Question

The decision to appeal is never an easy one. There are a lot of factors that go into this decision. For some of our clients, pursuing an appeal until they can appeal no more, irrespective of the time it takes or the cost required, is a matter of principle. They see the appeal as more than a part of the employment process. They may believe they have been slandered or otherwise defamed by the allegations and charges against them. Sometimes they are right—sometimes, it just feels that way.

For other clients, they feel like they must challenge the discipline to stand up to a bully supervisor or unjust system. Their victory lies in the ability to have their say in an open forum, to allow their attorney to cross-examine their accuser, and to let all the facts come out. At times, this is enough even if the discipline stands. Sometimes the exposure of poor practices and unprofessional supervisors is enough to bring about changes in the agency.

At times, we also represent firefighters who appeal their discipline in the hopes of negotiating a lesser punishment. While this can be a risky strategy, we have been very successful with this path. When the firefighter files an appeal, the human resources department becomes directly involved. In addition, for the first time, an attorney representing the department or the government entity will typically become involved in the case. The attorney for the government entity represents the city without question, just as your attorney represents you. However, attorneys are trained to see the strengths and weaknesses in their case and the case of the other party. The introduction of another attorney brings the potential for your attorney to find a resolution acceptable to both you and your employer.

Sometimes the exposure of poor practices and unprofessional supervisors is enough to bring about changes in the agency.

Unless a third party, like a union or legal defense plan, is paying your legal fees and expenses, your ability to continue the appeal will, unfortunately, be affected by finances at some point. While there are opportunities to seek attorney fees through an appeal, those options are limited. You should be honest with your attorney about the cost of each level of appeal. These frank conversations will allow your attorney to seek and secure a resolution that will be acceptable to you and your family.

Appeals require a lot of work for you as well as for your attorney. Appendix I includes a Checklist for Your Disciplinary Appeal. It is by no means exhaustive, but should help and also convince you that every appeal requires a great deal of preparation.

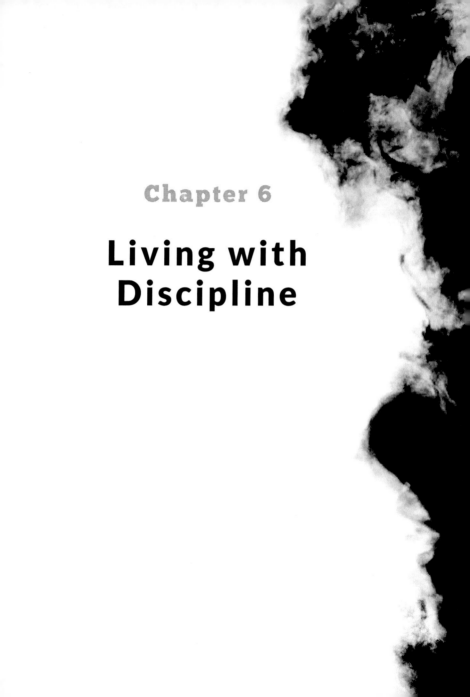

Chapter 6

Living with Discipline

I'll miss the guys,
but I'll do something else.

—Actual quote from a firefighter client
(more than one)

Discipline is difficult. It's hard for the supervisors who recommend and administer it, as well as for the firefighters who receive it. Discipline can improve performance and push people to exceed their potential, but it can also destroy morale and the motivation to advance in rank or even continue employment.

My firm has represented and consulted with a lot of employees facing or in receipt of discipline. While some were up front about their violations and understood some punishment was justified, most were either unclear about why they were being punished or concerned that the process lacked fairness. Although you can probably dismiss one or two of them as being intentionally ignorant or disgruntled, certainly not all of them were. In my opinion, many of them had legitimate concerns with the disciplinary process.

> *Discipline can improve performance and push people to exceed their potential, but it can also destroy morale and the motivation to advance in rank or even continue employment.*

FRONT-LINE STORY

We handled several cases from an agency that seems to write up a lot of people for "insubordination," which in one case included the employee reportedly letting out a sigh when advised of pending discipline.

We searched several years of discipline and discovered that an amazing number of employees were "insubordinate," but our client had received the longest suspension for a first offense. This was helpful information and supported the client's belief that the discipline was the result of a personal agenda.

What is the goal of discipline? Well, that depends upon who answers that question, which management book you read, and likely, whether the person responding was recently disciplined. Generally, all the management gurus agree that the goal of discipline is to correct behavior. Sometimes, the unintended consequences overshadow the goal.

Any supervisor must recognize three undeniable facts about discipline:

1. Discipline must be conducted in private with respect for the employee.
2. The more professional the delivery of the discipline, the more the action has a chance of being received as a constructive process. The opposite is also true.
3. A supervisor must be able to get past the discipline. In short, when it is complete, the supervisor must move ahead. If she does not, the employee will never do so.

Firefighters of any rank and tenure who receive discipline will feel a mix of emotions afterward. They may feel disappointed and angry at themselves and their chain of command. They may feel helpless and embarrassed, especially if the sanction included a loss of a position or rank. These strong emotions are hard to overcome in any context or environment. However, public safety professionals are different than private sector employees. Many times,

Management gurus agree that the goal of discipline is to correct behavior. Sometimes, the unintended consequences overshadow the goal.

they define themselves by their status as a firefighter. In addition, their friends and social groups may be largely composed of firefighters and their families. Being separated or distanced from that status and support group can be devastating. Public safety employees also wear their rank on display for all to see. Demotions are very public.

I've sat with so many public servants who have received discipline. Some appealed and won, others appealed and lost. Still others decided they did not want to publicly fight the decision of the department. Sadly, many of them were frightened of repercussions if they exercised their appeal rights or constitutional rights to call witnesses on their behalf. This should never be the case.

HOT TIP

Here is my recommendation for the firefighters reading this book. Make your decision about whether to appeal, commit to that course of action, and move on. What you do on a daily basis means more to your community, your family, and your neighbors than you can ever truly understand. Hold your head up when you go back to work, learn from the entire process, and be a better professional going forward.

After some twenty years representing public safety officers, I have represented young firefighters and LEOs facing discipline who are now senior command staff. Some of them serve in the same departments that administered that discipline so long ago, and others found a new home. All of them remained true to their servant hearts and focused upon the people they committed to serve.

Conclusion

Committing to a Better Profession

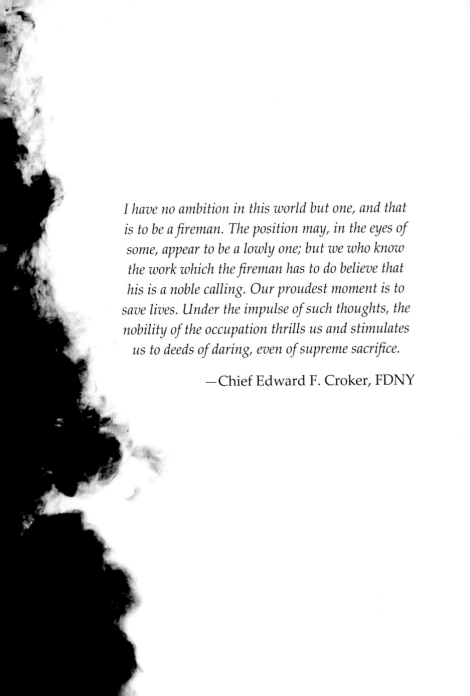

I have no ambition in this world but one, and that is to be a fireman. The position may, in the eyes of some, appear to be a lowly one; but we who know the work which the fireman has to do believe that his is a noble calling. Our proudest moment is to save lives. Under the impulse of such thoughts, the nobility of the occupation thrills us and stimulates us to deeds of daring, even of supreme sacrifice.

—Chief Edward F. Croker, FDNY

After over thirty years of wearing one badge or another and associating closely with public safety officers, I have never met a single one who went to work with anything but the best of intentions. Public safety is an honorable profession filled with dedicated professionals. Despite a few loud and often uninformed critics, the public overwhelmingly supports public safety. I have no doubt of that, and I have witnessed that support firsthand.

Now that we've come to the end of a book about administrative investigations and discipline, let's look forward to the future. Recruiting is down in all public safety professions. Shifts are short-handed, many departments have implemented mandatory overtime rules, and senior firefighters are retiring as soon as they are eligible. As you read this book, you are part of the future of public safety in the United States.

While I'm in the process of publishing this book, firefighters and other first responders are putting themselves at risk every day while the rest of America is sheltering in place during the COVID-19 pandemic crisis. You should be very proud of the fact that no one in the public, even your critics, ever expected that you would stay at home and refuse to work.

I recently pondered a question I believe is appropriate to explore at this point in the book: When we spend so much time recruiting people into public safety, training them, and indoctrinating them into the profession and culture of public service, why can we not seem to go a week without taking pay away from those very same people through discipline? Below is an article I wrote for PoliceOne.com. It focuses on this very question. Many of you are supervisors and command staff, and the rest of you likely will be in the future. I hope this article helps put the role of administrative investigations and discipline into focus.

10 Steps to Lowering the Rate of Public Sector Discipline and Avoiding Lawsuits[53]
by Lance J. LoRusso, Esq.

I am honored to represent several thousand Georgia law enforcement officers and firefighters. My firm has represented more than seventy officers following shootings or in-custody deaths. We handle employment, licensing board, and disciplinary appeals. Prior to staring my career in law enforcement in 1988, I worked in the private sector in the hospitality industry. As an attorney since 1999, I have represented corporations including one with 22,000 employees as well as private and public sector employees. These companies seem to be able to function, under stressful circumstances and quite efficiently, without writing up, suspending, and firing employees on a regular basis.

Lately I find myself asking, "Why are so many LEOs and firefighters written up, suspended, and fired?" This is a critical question when law enforcement and firefighters are having a difficult time recruiting and retaining talent.

The private sector in the United States employs almost 127 million people.[54] Firefighters and law enforcement officers total approximately 1.8 million.[55] However, it is a notable and relatively rare event for private sector employees to be suspended or even written up, much less terminated.

Private sector employees may receive, on the high end, a day or two of orientation and an employee manual. Police and fire recruits receive hundreds of hours of training with minimum standards and voluminous SOP manuals for their agency, codes of conduct, and government employee manuals. So, why can't they seem to go a week without suspending or firing a LEO or firefighter? Apparently, more training does not equal less discipline.

Is it the difficulty and stress of the work performed? Probably not. Private sector employees work on extremely strict deadlines with performance pressure, and companies may fail if the employees perform poorly. Public sector employees are called upon to make "split-second judgments in circumstances that are tense, uncertain, and rapidly evolving,"[56] and that mountain of manuals, memos, and guidelines may take a backseat to intuition, improvisation, and bravery. A private sector employee who thinks outside the box will likely be rewarded with a bigger bonus, while a public sector employee may be rewarded with a counseling session or time off without pay even though they cannot predict their schedules, their duties, or the people who stand in the way of their success on a daily basis.

The "we hold public sector employees to a higher standard" theory fails as well. That's an excuse and is generally not true. For example, courtesy toward the people served is critical in both environments. The difference lies in how violations are handled. A rude receptionist will receive more training, a counseling session, and be monitored more closely. Discipline, including termination, may occur if these remedial steps do not correct the problem. However, a rude officer risks being suspended or terminated irrespective of the manner in which they were treated on the scene by their "customer." The private sector does not view the receptionist as a disposable commodity or view the taking of money from an employee's paycheck as a first-level solution. The public sector does.

It is astonishing that this continues in an environment where law enforcement agencies and fire and emergency services are fighting a war of attrition and sagging recruiting. According to an NBC article poll, law enforcement recruiting is down all over the United States.

Although this might reduce my caseload, here are my recommendations:

1. If several people commit the same violation, it's either a training, supervision, or management problem. Fix the underlying problem.
2. Most errors are the result of inadequate training or communication. Use your internal investigations to get to the root cause of the problem. The medical field and airline industry use root cause analyses to understand *why* a rule or policy violation occurred. Too many internal investigations are solely focused on an end goal of catching people in a policy violation.
3. Make taking pay away from the people you recruited, selected, trained, work to retain, and in whom you *invested* thousands of dollars and your trust the last resort.
4. NEVER be flippant or casual about suspending or firing someone. Snide remarks like "a few days off would do them some good" or "we'll just hire another one to take his place" evidence

nothing but arrogance or ignorance, not leadership. Never forget that officer or firefighter must explain to a spouse or child why their paycheck is short. Take it seriously, or take yourself out of the equation.

5. Ensure your process to suspend or terminate someone is fair, thorough, and free from personal bias. My principal piece of advice to command-level public sector employees is simple. NEVER fire or discipline someone when you are angry, having a bad day, or tired. You can always fire them tomorrow.

6. Have the courage to listen when people in your organization are screaming for help about a supervisor or manager. Public sector employees understand fairness—they are the guardians of due process and discretion when enforcing the law. One bad supervisor or manager can destroy an agency, deflate morale, and get you and your agency sued—successfully.

7. Expect employees to make mistakes. Rare is the person who makes errors born of malice.

8. Take exit interviews seriously and follow up to get details. I have seen things that are nothing short of horrible, like one personnel file that grew by over sixty pages *after* the officer resigned. Amazing and inexcusable.

9. Take "name-clearing sessions," "pre-disciplinary

hearings," and Loudermill hearings seriously. Listen to what people say and *encourage* them to speak. Whether required or not, these proceedings are the last opportunity for your agency to learn of a serious problem. I have successfully sued agencies that ignored the opportunity to address issues and prevent the lawsuit by listening prior to taking adverse action.

10. Communicate with people openly and do not let the "chain of command" get in the way of common sense. I have unfortunately seen the chain of command used as a weapon when an employee was justifiably seeking help because they were being treated poorly, and at times in an unlawful manner, by a supervisor.

There is too much at stake in keeping good, caring, competent, dedicated, brave, and honest public servants on the street. It's not about egos or the time it will take to do things differently. It takes a few minutes to write an order suspending someone. It takes longer to perform a root cause analysis to determine why the behavior or incident took place.

Agencies that practice these principles have better recruiting, better retention, and better morale than their peers. If these reasons don't convince you, they are also sued less often.

Change takes time and effort. Your officers and fire-fighters deserve your time and effort. I've told many journalists during interviews when they are ready to bash law enforcement, "If you don't like the current crop of law enforcement officers, wait until you see the second string when recruiting standards drop in order to fill positions." There's too much at stake to keep doing things "the way we've always done it." Stay safe.

***

I hope this article spoke to you. I sincerely believe the culture and manner of discipline in public safety must change.

This book has taken you on a sometimes difficult journey from the first hint of an OPS investigation through the investigative process, a review of your rights, what to expect from the process, how to appeal, when to continue your appeal, and living with discipline. Most importantly, I discussed the role of an attorney as your trusted advisor. OPS investigations are a part of public sector employment. Like any other inevitable process, you must be prepared and face them with confidence.

The most important resources at any fire department are the people who work there to serve the public, and the most important decisions are those that affect the lives of those people. Discipline and investigations are serious and have lasting effects that can change the course of lives and families. We all owe the public our very best efforts to ensure our firefighters are trained well and treated fairly.

Thank you for taking the time to read this book, to consider that one day you may be faced with discipline, and to prepare yourself for that day. Stay true to the oath you took, serve the public, and be proud every day that you wear the badge and uniform of a firefighter.

APPENDICES

Appendix A

SAMPLE NOTICE OF INVESTIGATION

XXXXXXX Fire and Rescue Department

Officer of Professional Standards

XXXXXX Elm Street

XXXXXXXXXX, XXXXXXX

Firefighter XXXXXXX:

Pursuant to Policy No. XXXXX, you are hereby notified that you are the subject of an internal investigation regarding your conduct as a City of XXXXX Firefighter. As a city employee, you have certain rights. Should you have any questions about these rights, you should refer to the City Policy Manual and the department SOP.

Your interview will take place at XXXX hours on September XX, 20XX. Should you need to reschedule this meeting, you must contact Investigator XXXXXX immediately. The Office of Professional Responsibility will work to accommodate timely requests, if possible. However, your appearance is mandatory and you can be ordered to appear.

You are instructed not to discuss this letter or investigation with anyone except as needed to schedule your appearance or to consult with legal counsel or a union representative.

Call Investigator XXXXX with any questions.

Appendix B

CHECKLIST FOR YOUR OPS INTERVIEW

1. Know the time and date of the interview. Do not be late!

2. Do not work the night before an interview.

3. Get as much sleep as possible prior to answering questions.

4. Dress in your clean, well-pressed uniform or professional business attire. Think about attending the most important job interview of your career and dress appropriately.

5. Ask for a copy of the allegations.

6. Ask for the specifics of the charges or policies you are accused of violating.

7. Gather AND review any related incident reports or other materials about which you may be questioned.

8. Meet with your attorney at least a week prior, if possible.

9. Meet with your attorney the day prior to follow up on any newly discovered information or information recently disclosed by your department.

10. Make certain you know where to park. When firefighters are placed on administrative leave, particularly without pay, their parking cards are often deactivated or collected. You may be forced to use public parking facilities, making it more difficult to find a space or increase your travel time to arrive early.

11. Give your attorney some guidance on parking.

12. Find a nearby location to have a private, last-minute conversation with your attorney.

13. Avoid discussing the case with your attorney in restrooms, elevators, hallways, parking garages, or anywhere you cannot be absolutely certain you have privacy.

14. Avoid conversations with people in your department as you arrive and walk to the OPS office. You may not have seen some of these coworkers for a while. This is especially true if you have been on administrative leave. Make polite conversation, talk about the weather, your children, a ball game, etc. If they ask about your case, just reply that things are moving along or something to that effect.

15. Let your attorney know if anything comes up at the last minute, such as a childcare issue, a family emergency, or you are not feeling well. It is better to have your attorney contact OPS to let the investigator know, as it will look less like an excuse to avoid or delay the OPS interview.

16. Review the documents and materials you have to prepare for the OPS interview.

17. Prepare to take time to answer questions. The questions may be difficult, may relate to incidents that occurred a long time ago, or may just require you to think before you answer.

18. Get comfortable with the fact that you cannot, and SHOULD not, rush through the interview. Although the process may be uncomfortable, you are required to give *complete* and accurate answers. If you rush, you will likely forget something.

19. Write down the facts, dates, times, or other details that are either extremely important or difficult for you to remember.

20. Remember that this is an investigation and, by nature, an adversarial process. The level of discomfort depends upon the style of the investigator. However, if you are facing discipline, do not expect a warm and fuzzy, casual conversation.

Appendix C

SAMPLE GARRITY WARNINGS[57]

XXXXXXXX Fire Department

Office of Professional Standards

Internal Affairs

This GARRITY WARNING is being administered consistent with an Internal Administrative Investigation consistent with *Garrity v. New Jersey*, 385 U.S. 493 87 S. CT. 616 (1967) and *Uniformed Sanitation Men Association, Inc. Et. Al. v. Commissioner of Sanitation of the City of New York, Et. Al.*, 392 U.S.

You are being questioned as part of an official, internal administrative investigation which is being conducted on behalf of the City by an investigator who is a designee of the Fire Chief.

You will be asked questions specifically directed and narrowly related to the performance of your official duties and/or fitness for office. You are entitled to all of the rights and privileges guaranteed by the Constitution and Laws of the State and the Constitution of the

United States of America, including the right not to be compelled to incriminate yourself.

You are advised that if you should refuse to testify or answer any questions relating to the performance of your official duties and/or fitness for office, you shall be subject to departmental charges which could result in disciplinary action or termination of employment.

Neither your statements nor any information or evidence which is gained by reason of such statements can be used as evidence against you in any subsequent criminal proceeding **(except for perjury or obstruction of justice charges)**. However, these statements and any information or evidence which is gained by reason of such statements can be used against you in subsequent departmental charges.

_____ _____ _____
Employee Name (print)   **Signature**   **Date**

_____ _____ _____
Investigator Name (print)   **Signature**   **Date**

XXXXXXX FIRE DEPARTMENT

Garrity Advisory

To: —————————————————

Date: —————————————————

From: —————————————————

Subject: Administrative Investigation of Employee Misconduct

I/A Case Number(s): —————————————

Allegations of employee misconduct must be taken seriously by all concerned. All complainants are warned that to knowingly give false statements may result in criminal prosecution. As an employee, you need to understand that for you to refuse to truthfully answer questions relating to the performance of your official duties and/or fitness for duty will result in disciplinary action up to, and including, termination of employment for the violations of D.O.M. Chapter 5, Section C, Standards of Conduct, #2 *Insubordination* and/or

D.O.M. Chapter 5, Section C, Standards of Conduct, #25 *Internal Affairs.*

You will be asked questions specifically directed and closely related to the performance of your official duties and/or fitness for office. You do not have the right to have an attorney present during this administrative proceeding. The Internal Affairs Section will record the interview and a copy of the recording may be obtained once a disposition has been made. If an employee surreptitiously records the interview, they will be subject to disciplinary action up to, and including, termination of employment for the violations of entitled D.O.M. Chapter 5, Section C, Standards of Conduct, #2 *Insubordination.* Depending on the nature of the Administrative Investigation, the Fire Chief or their designee may require you to submit to a polygraph examination, participate in a lineup, be photographed, submit financial disclosure statements, and/or submit to a medical examination. However, neither the statement(s) nor evidence you provide for this Administrative Investigation can be used against you in a criminal proceeding, except for perjury or obstruction of justice.

Above all, please remember that these investigations are designed to protect many interests, including your own. The investigations also identify problems in policies or training, the correction of which will benefit all of us.

Your cooperation in this investigation does not constitute a waiver of any appeal, grievance, or other legal right(s). Until a final disposition has been rendered, and the case formally closed, you are hereby ordered not to discuss this investigation with anyone other than personnel assigned to the Internal Affairs Unit. (This does not preclude the right of an employee to consult with an attorney or representative of his/her choice at a time other than during an administrative interview.)

I have read and understand the above information.

_____   _____
Witness Signature   **Employee Signature**

_____   _____
Witness Signature   **Date Time**

Appendix D

SAMPLE KALKINES WARNINGS

ADVICE OF RIGHTS (KALKINES)

You are going to be asked a number of specific questions concerning the performance of your official duties as it relates to:

Under the provisions of the Inspector General Act, 5 U.S.C.A. App. 3, as amended, you are required to cooperate fully by disclosing complete and accurate information pertaining to matters under OIG review.

You may be subject to disciplinary action, to include termination, for refusing to provide information or answer questions posed by OIG officials if questioned on a matter that may lead only to an administrative action (as distinct from a criminal prosecution).

You are advised that the answers you provide pertaining to the matter presently under investigation, or any information or evidence which is gained by reason of your answers, cannot and will not be used against you in a criminal proceeding, except that you may be subject to criminal prosecution for any false statements made during this interview.

I have read the aforementioned and agree to the terms mentioned therein.

_____   _____

Signature   (Date/Time)

_____

Print Name

KALKINES WARNING

This administrative interview being conducted by _____ and _____ related to the official business of the United States XXXXXXXX Police.

Being interviewed is _____ _____. This interview is being mechanically recorded and will become an official record of the United States XXXXXXXX Police.

You are being asked to provide information as part of an investigation being conducted by the United States XXXXXXXX Police into an alleged misconduct or improper performance of official duties. The investigation involves IAU #_____.

The purpose of this interview is to obtain information which will assist in the determination of whether administrative action is warranted.

You are going to be asked a number of specific questions concerning the performance of your official duties.

You have a duty to reply to these questions, and agency disciplinary actions, including dismissal, may be undertaken if you refuse to answer, or fail to reply fully and truthfully.

The answers you furnish and any information or evidence resulting therefrom may be used in the course of civil or administrative proceedings.

Neither your answers nor any information or evidence which is gained by reason of such statements can be used against you in any criminal proceedings, except that if you knowingly and willfully provide false statements or information in your answers, you may be criminally prosecuted for that action.

_____   _____   _____
Employee Signature   Location   Date

_____   _____
Investigator/Witness Signature   Date

SAMPLE WEINGARTEN RIGHTS FORM

WEINGARTEN RIGHTS FORM

Weingarten Rights are mandated by law, and materialized from an actual case (*National Labor Relations Board v. J. Weingarten, Inc.*) decided by the US Supreme Court in 1975. The rights announced by the Court are as follows:

Employees have the right to request that a representative be present at any investigatory meeting when the employee reasonably believes that disciplinary action might result from the investigation.

PROCESS

1. The employee may request a representative prior to the meeting or at any time during the meeting.

2. If the meeting is delayed or interrupted at the employee's request for a representative, then

the meeting and subsequent questions should end and one of the following decisions must be reached:

- Reschedule the meeting to allow a representative to attend. A reasonable time period should be allowed.

- Move forward with the investigation and take appropriate action without information from the employee.

- Inform the employee that he/she has a choice to either voluntarily give up his/her rights to a representative and meet, or the meeting may or may not be rescheduled and the employee's information not considered in the investigation.

REPRESENTATIVE'S ROLE

1. A representative, if requested, must be given the opportunity to meet with the employee prior to the meeting.

2. During the meeting, a representative may ask for clarification of questions, but may not tell the employee what to say.

3. Employee/Representative may request to consult in private during this meeting.

INVOKEMENT OF WEINGARTEN RIGHTS

❑ I choose to invoke my Weingarten Rights and request that a representative be present at the investigatory meeting.

❑ I do not request to invoke my Weingarten Rights.

ACKNOWLEDGMENT OF RECEIPT OF YOUR WEINGARTEN RIGHTS

I,_____, have had full opportunity to read and consider the contents of this form, and I understand that, by signing this form, I am confirming the receipt of my Weingarten Rights, as described in this form.

_____   _____

Signature   Date

YOU ARE ENTITLED TO A COPY OF THIS FORM AFTER YOU SIGN IT.

Appendix F

SAMPLE NOTICE OF PROPOSED DISCIPLINE

From: A/C S. G. Sample
Thru: D/C D. B. Smith
       Batt. Chief M. T. Jones
       Capt. P. F. Green
       Lt. R. T. Gray
To: FIREFIGHTER H. M. Blass
Date: April 13, 20XX
Re: Proposed Termination

The Office of Professional Responsibility has completed its investigation concerning the allegations against you. As you are aware, on September 2, 20XX, you were formally charged with the following violations of the Code of Conduct, the City Policy, and the Departmental Policy Manual:

       XXXXXXXX
       XXXXXXXX
       XXXXXXXX

The command staff has considered the findings and information obtained by the Office of Professional

Standards. I have considered your X years of service to the city, the severity of the pending charges, and your disciplinary history as set out below:

September 20XX	*Tardiness*	*8-hour suspension*
April 20XX	*Insubordination*	*24-hour suspension*

Based upon the totality of the circumstances and the department's history of how similar violations have been punished in the past, I am recommending your termination.

Pursuant to City Policy No. 45-672, you may provide additional information or a statement in person or in writing to Chief Trover prior to the final imposition of discipline. Any statement in writing must be received on or before Tuesday April 20, 20XX. Should you wish to appeal in person, you must notify me via email before 1700 hours on April 14, 20XX.

If you wish to appear in person, the meeting must take place before 1700 hours on April 20, 20XX. You will be afforded an opportunity to speak and present witnesses. The meeting is limited to two hours. You may have a representative or legal counsel present; however, they will not be permitted to participate.

Copy: Chief J. S. Trover
Bob Forrest, Director of Human Resources
Horace Gumper, City Manager

Appendix G

SAMPLE DISCIPLINE NOTICE WITH APPEAL OPTIONS

MEMORANDUM

From: Chief J. S. Trover
Thru: A/C S. G. Sample
D/C D. B. Smith
      Batt. Chief M. T. Jones
      Capt. P. F. Green
      Lt. R. T. Gray
To: FIREFIGHTER H. M. Blass
Date: April 23, 20XX
Re: Termination

On April 20, 20XX, you attended a meeting in my office pursuant to City Policy No. 45-672. You were accompanied by your attorney, who attended the proceedings as an observer only. During the meeting, you were permitted to present information and evidence in rebuttal or mitigation of the recommendation of your termination.

I considered the information you provided on April 20, 20XX. I also considered the findings and information obtained by the Office of Professional Standards, your X years of service to the city, the severity of the pending charges, your disciplinary history, and the department's history of how similar violations have been punished in the past. At this time, I am terminating your employment.

As a city employee, you have certain appeal rights concerning my decision to terminate your employment. I refer you to City Policy No. 45-224 for a full explanation of those rights. Attached to this letter, you will find a copy of this policy.

If you choose to appeal this termination, you MUST file a *written* appeal within ten (10) days of the date of this letter.

Copy: Bob Forrest, Director of Human Resources
         Horace Gumper, City Manager

Appendix H

SAMPLE APPEAL NOTIFICATIONS

Via Certified United States Mail, facsimile to 999-582-9595, and email to TroverJ@cityofflux.ga.gov

April 28, 20XX
Chief J. S. Trover
City of Flux Fire and Rescue Department
111 Main Street
Flux, GA 30999

Re: Appeal of Firefighter H. M. Blass

Dear Chief Trover,

I am writing to introduce myself as counsel for Firefighter H. M. Blass. Pursuant to City Policy No. 45-224, please accept this letter as formal and timely notification of her intent to appeal her termination from the City of Flux Fire and Rescue Department.

Please also consider this a formal request for the following documents pursuant to the Georgia Open Records Act, O.C.G.A. Section 50-18-70, et seq. As you are aware, you are required to respond to this request and provide specific reasons why any documents are being withheld or are not subject to release.

1. A complete, certified copy of any and all files, recordings, documents, or other materials involved in any way in the internal or administrative investigation connected to this termination;
2. Any and all emails, memoranda, letters, text messages, or other communications referencing or in any way connected to this termination;
3. A copy of any and all policies, rules, regulations, standard operating procedures, or other guidelines concerning:
   a. The appeal of this discipline;
   b. Release of records pursuant to the Georgia Open Records Act;
   c. The investigation of the facts giving rise to this discipline;
   d. The charges against Firefighter H. M. Blass;
4. All personnel and Office of Professional Standards (OPS) files concerning Firefighter H. M. Blass; and
5. A complete list of any and all City of Flux employees charged with similar infractions in the past ten (10) years.

Please contact me in advance if the costs of retrieving and copying the above-referenced documents will exceed $100. We respectfully request that you produce documents in electronic format whenever possible.

As you have been advised that Firefighter H. M. Blass is represented by counsel, I must insist that no one from your agency or the City of Flux have any contact with her whatsoever. Any communications or requests must go through my firm.

Please contact me with any questions or concerns. I look forward to working with you through this process. You may reach me at the numbers above or via email at lance@lorussolawfirm.com.

Sincerely,
Lance J. LoRusso, Esq.

MEMORANDUM[58]

From: FIREFIGHTER H. M. Blass
To: Chief J. S. Trover
Date: April 28, 20XX
Re: Appeal of termination

Pursuant to City Policy No. 45-224, please accept this as a timely notice of my intention to seek an appeal to my termination. Please contact me at 999-867-5309 or IMABLASS@provider.com.

Copy: Bob Forrest, Director of Human Resources
Horace Gumper, City Manager

Appendix I

CHECKLIST FOR YOUR DISCIPLINARY APPEAL

1. Do you have all the documents necessary to understand the appeal process?

2. Does your attorney have the policies and procedures that outline your appeal process?

3. Have you calendared the deadline to file the appeal?

4. Are you clear on how the appeal must be filed?

5. Have you considered the alternatives to an appeal, such as negotiating toward a better outcome?

6. Do you have copies of the investigation to understand the evidence against you?

7. Are you clear on what you are seeking through the appeal—reversal of a termination, a lessened penalty, retirement or resignation in lieu of discipline, or a letter in your file explaining any mitigating circumstances that were not brought out in the appeal?

8. What is your status pending the appeal—leave with or

without pay, terminated, full duty, modified duty, on work restrictions that prevent part-time or extra jobs?

9. Who are the witnesses you will need to prove your case?

10. What documents will you need to prove your case?

NOTES

1. This figure (373,600 career firefighters, 682,600 volunteers) is based on the NFPA 2016 National Fire Experience Survey. See Ben Evarts & Gary Stein, U.S. Fire Department Profile, p.3, National Fire Protection Association (March 2019), retrieved from https://www.nfpa.org/-/media/Files/News-and-Research/Fire-statistics-and-reports/Emergency-responders/osfdprofile.pdf.
2. "NFPA statistics – Fire department calls," retrieved November 24, 2019, https://www.nfpa.org/News-and-Research/Data-research-and-tools/Emergency-Responders/Fire-department-calls.
3. The mean hourly wage. See 33-2011 Firefighters, Occupational Employment and Wages, US Bureau of Labor Statistics (May 2018), retrieved from https://www.bls.gov/oes/current/oes332011.htm.
4. The top 90 percent hourly wage. See 33-2011 Firefighters, Occupational Employment and Wages, US Bureau of Labor Statistics (May 2018), retrieved from https://www.bls.gov/oes/current/oes332011.htm.
5. PTSD is a disorder. PTS is a normal, human response to severe stress or exposure to severely stressful events.
6. Progressive discipline policies set forth a type of escalation of consequences, from verbal reprimand through termination. They typically allow for management to bypass the "steps" in the process, depending upon the severity of the violation.
7. Management always benefits from explicit education regarding

appeal procedures and due process. This is one of the critical methods to preventing discrimination lawsuits.

8. A policy or custom "can be either a written custom or policy, such as an ordinance, or an unwritten practice that is so widespread and 'so permanent and well settled as to constitute a custom or use with the force of law.'" *Flowers v. Patrick*, 869 F. Supp. 2d 1331, 1334–35 (M.D. Ala. 2012) (quoting *City of St. Louis v. Praprotnik*, 485 U.S. 112, 127, 108 S. Ct. 915, 99 L. Ed. 2d 107 (1988)).

9. Law enforcement officer. This term encompasses every type, level, and rank of sworn person who carries a badge and gun and makes arrests.

10. Although the catchall "conduct unbecoming" is often used, there is a burden of proof associated with that charge as well as every other.

11. Employees may also have an individual contract that governs the rights or obligations of both the employee and their employer. However, these are uncommon except at the level of the appointed fire chief.

12. This also means that a person can work without being a member of a union.

13. This is usually done with a statement similar to this: "The parties agree this contract shall be governed by the policies, charter, or rules of the government entity in existence at the time it is executed."

14. "Had the employment contract been inconsistent with the policies and procedures, the employment agreement, by its terms, would take precedence." *Marias Healthcare Servs. v. Turenne*, 2001 MT 127, ¶ 20, 305 Mont. 419, 424, 28 P.3d 491, 496.

15. *Cleveland Bd. of Ed v. Loudermill*, 470 U.S. 572 (1985).

16. Due process is "flexible and calls for such procedural protections as the particular situation demands." *Gilbert v. Homar*, 520 U.S. 924, 930 (1997).

17. "But the Constitution sets a floor for the protection of individual rights. The constitutional floor is sturdy and often high, but it is

a floor. Other federal, state, and local government entities generally possess authority to safeguard individual rights above and beyond the rights secured by the U.S. Constitution." See *Am. Legion v. Am. Humanist Ass'n*, 139 S. Ct. 2067 (2019).

18. *Miranda v. Arizona*, 384 U.S. 436 (1966).

19. *Self-incrimination*: No person shall be compelled to give testimony tending in any manner to be self-incriminating. Ga. Const. Art. I, §I. Para. VVI.

20. Per the parallel postulate, also called Euclid's fifth postulate because it is the fifth postulate in Euclid's *Elements*. This is a distinctive axiom in Euclidean geometry. You now know all the math I know. Lawyers do not do math, but Sister Imelda would be proud.

21. *Garrity v. State of N.J.*, 385 U.S. 493, 479 (1967).

22. 288 Ga. 165 (2010).

23. *Weingarten* provides a right to have a representative present if a member of a collective bargaining unit is subject to investigation. *N.L.R.B. v. Weingarten*, 420 U.S. 251 (1975).

24. *Lingler v. Fechko*, 312 F.3d 237, 239 (6th Cir. 2002).

25. The United States Court of Claims was established in 1855 to hear claims against the United States. Opinions were directly appealable to the United States Supreme Court. The court was abolished in 1982 and jurisdiction was transferred to the United States Court of Federal Claims. Appellate jurisdiction for the court now lies with United States Court of Appeals for the Federal Circuit.

26. *Kalkines v. United States*, 473 F.2d 1391 (Ct. Cl. 1973) (amended on rehearing).

27. The Court of Claims reviewed the transcripts of the recorded interviews.

28. *Kalkines*, 473 F.2d at 1396–97.

29. *Kalkines*, 473 F.2d at 1396. Emphasis added.

30. *Kalkines*, 473 F.2d at 1395–96. Emphasis added.

31. *Miranda v. Arizona*, 384 U.S. 436 (1966); *Dickerson v. US*, 530 U.S. 428 (2000).

32. *Kalkines*, 473 F.2d at 1397.
33. "Immunity . . . may be involvement can be independently proven. A more limited immunity, 'use and derivative use' immunity, protects the witness from the use of either the incriminating testimony or the fruits of such testimony." *State v. Hanson*, 249 Ga. 739, 741, 295 S.E.2d 297, 300 (1982).
34. *Kalkines*, 473 F.2d at 1398. Emphasis added.
35. *Kalkines*, 473 F.2d at 1393. Emphasis added.
36. "Accordingly, we hold that a police officer may be dismissed for just cause within the meaning of R.C. 4141.29(D)(2)(a) when he or she refuses to obey a superior's reasonable order to take a polygraph test, so long as the officer has been informed as part of such order (1) of the subject of the intended inquiry, which is specifically and narrowly related to the performance of the officer's official duties, (2) that the officer's answers cannot be used against him or her in any subsequent criminal prosecution, and (3) that the penalty for such is dismissal." *City of Warrensville Heights v. Jennings*, 569 N.E.2d 489, 494 (OH 1991).
37. This is a complex area of law. You should consult with an attorney before letting any appeal deadline approach or pass.
38. I discussed the origin and scope of *Garrity* protections in Chapter 3.
39. Remember that criminal charges can generally be brought anytime within the applicable statute of limitations. This may be up to four years, which is far longer than most agencies have to investigate misconduct. Allegations of lying during a sworn statement to OPS investigators can give rise to criminal charges, even in an OPS interview that was given under *Garrity* protection.
40. USCS Fed Rules Evid R 602 (witness needs personal knowledge); USCS Fed Rules Evid R 612 (use of a writing to refresh recollection, as long as the writing is shown to the adverse party if used to refresh at trial).
41. *Garrity v. State of N.J.*, 385 U.S. 493 (1967).
42. "Other courts that have addressed this issue have held that a

police officer has no Sixth Amendment right to counsel at an internal affairs interview or similar administrative proceeding where loss of liberty is not threatened. See, e.g., *Los Angeles Police Protective League v. Gates*, 579 F. Supp. 36, 41 (C.D. Cal. 1984) (holding that Sixth Amendment right to counsel did not apply because no loss of liberty was threatened); *Wilson v. Swing*, 463 F. Supp. 555, 560–561 (M.D.N.C. 1978) (finding that Sixth Amendment right to counsel did not attach because proceeding was purely civil in nature)." *Gray v. Bexar Cty. Sheriff's Civil Serv. Comm'n*, No. 97-50170, 1997 U.S. App. LEXIS 42055, at *9 (5th Cir. Oct. 13, 1997).

"The Sixth Amendment right to effective assistance of counsel is a criminal concept with no relevance to administrative or civil proceedings. This observation was correct; the Sixth Amendment right to effective assistance of counsel did not apply to the appellant's non-criminal, administrative discharge hearing." *Williams v. Wynne*, 533 F.3d 360, 369 (5th Cir. 2008).

43. "Counsel . . . my interpose objection to questions put to the officer by the interrogator and, further, may consult with the officer only to the extent necessary to make a particular objection. All other consultation, if any, should occur prior to the interrogation. In that respect, the interrogation differs naught from the taking of a deposition in a civil case." *Nichols v. Balt. Police Dep't*, 53 Md. App. 623, 629 (1983).

"Nichols declares his 14th Amendment Due Process rights have been violated because counsel or the representative can do no more than object. Although the appellant likens the IID (Internal Investigation Division) to a grand jury, the analogy falls far short of the mark because the IID interrogation is, in appellant's case, strictly non-criminal. So long as no criminal charge emanates from the interrogation, there is no violation of the officer's 14th Amendment Due Process Right. *Garrity v. New Jersey*, 385 U.S. 493, 87 S.Ct. 616, 17 L.Ed.2d 562 (1967). See also *Gardner v. Broderick*, 392 U.S. 273 (1968) and *Uniformed Sanitation Men Association v. Commissioner of Sanitation*, 392 U.S.

280 (1968)." *Nichols v. Balt. Police Dep't*, 53 Md. App. 623, 629–30 (1983).

44. Where an employee's statements are immunized from use in future criminal proceedings, they can be discharged if they refuse to answer the interview questions. *Uniformed Sanitation Men Association v. Commissioner of Sanitation*, 392 U.S. 280 (1968). But see *Gardner v. Broderick*, 392 U.S. 273 (1969) (employee cannot be fired or disciplined *solely* upon assertion of Fifth Amendment right).

45. Though the National Labor Relations Act's collective bargaining laws do not apply to government employees, many states have enacted legislation governing collective bargaining agreements for public employees. The legislation is usually accompanied by Public Employee Relations Boards to enforce the legislation. For a list of states with Public Employee Relations Boards, visit www.nrtw.org/national-right-to-work-public-employee-relations-boards (last visited January 30, 2020).

Courts have generally held that disciplinary procedures for public employees are proper subjects for collective bargaining agreements. POLICE UNION CONTRACTS, 66 Duke L.J. 1191, 1206. See, e.g., *City of Casselberry v. Orange Cty. Police Benevolent Ass'n*, 482 So. 2d 336, 340 (Fla. 1986) (holding that even though the state civil service law established some procedures for demotion and discharge, municipalities were still required to bargain collectively on those issues to the extent necessary to potentially establish alternate grievance procedures); *City of Reno v. Reno Police Protective Ass'n*, 653 P.2d 156, 158 (Nev. 1982) (holding that Nevada law requires municipalities to negotiate with police departments over disciplinary measures); *Union Twp. Bd. of Trs. v. Fraternal Order of Police*, Ohio Valley Lodge No. 112, 766 N.E.2d 1027, 1031–32 (Ohio Ct. App. 2001) (holding that discipline was a mandatory subject of bargaining, so that when the township refused to bargain, a conciliator could select the union's proposal on discipline in its final settlement award).

However, some states have adopted statutes similar to

the National Labor Relations Act. As a result, such states have adopted the US Supreme Court's decision in *Weingarten*, which holds that an employee has the right to a "union representative" upon the employee's request during an investigatory interview where the employee reasonably believes discipline might result. See *NLRB v. J. Weingarten, Inc.*, 420 U.S. 251, 260, 95 S. Ct. 959, 965 (1975); see also *Cheltenham Twp. v. Pa. Labor Rels. Bd.*, 846 A.2d 173, 176 (Pa. Commw. Ct. 2004). Thus, the right to representation does not extend to the right to counsel in such states. See *Cheltenham Twp. v. Pa. Labor Rels. Bd.*, 846 A.2d 173, 179 (Pa. Commw. Ct. 2004) ("an 'outside representative' attending a *Weingarten* interview who happens to be an attorney can attend the interview, but cannot act as the individual's 'attorney'").

46. LEOs in stressful training exercises were unable to recall their path away from a threat when interviewed at the conclusion of the training. William J. Lewinski, Jennifer L. Dysterheft, Matthew M. Priem, and Robert W. Pettitt, "Police officers' actual vs. recalled path of travel in response to a threatening traffic stop scenario," *Police Practice and Research: An International Journal* 17 (2014): 1–17.

47. I am also licensed to practice law in Arkansas and Tennessee.

48. Most, if not all, states have administrative procedure acts, which govern hearings that occur outside of formal court settings. Check your state or ask your attorney for more information. See e.g. O.C.G.A. § 50-13-1.

49. I serve as an adjunct professor at Columbus State University and teach in the Georgia Command College.

50. Many times, the attorney can be present but may not speak. If this occurs, the firefighter will have to raise the issue. It may be advisable for the attorney and the firefighter to write out any technical challenges to ensure the issue is raised in an accurate and efficient manner.

51. Klepal, D., "Atlanta Workers Wait Months for Appeal Hearings," *Atlanta Journal-Constitution*, June 18, 2016.

52. This may involve a firefighter certification, an Emergency

Medical Technician certificate, or a paramedic license. Often these matters are handled by different state agencies.

53. Reprinted with express permission. https://www.policeone.com/legal/articles/483141006-10-steps-to-lowering-the-rate-of-public-sector-discipline-and-avoiding-lawsuits.

54. See US Census Bureau, 2016 SUSB Annual Data Sets: U.S. and States Totals, https://www.census.gov/data/tables/2016/econ/susb/2016-susb-annual.html (last revised July 29, 2019).

55. The numbers are a total estimate from the year 2017 for law enforcement officers and the year 2015 for firefighters. See Federal Bureau of Investigation, Criminal Justice Information Services Division, Uniform Crime Reporting Program: 2017 Crime in the United States – Table 70, https://ucr.fbi.gov/crime-in-the-u.s/2017/crime-in-the-u.s.-2017/topic-pages/tables/table-70 (indicating 670,279 sworn officers with a total of 13,128 law enforcement agencies reporting in 2017); see also National Fire Protection Association, The U.S. Fire Department Profile Through 2015 Fact Sheet, https://www.nfpa.org/-/media/Files/News-and-Research/Fire-statistics-and-reports/Fact-sheets/fd-profilefactsheet.pdf (indicating 1,160,450 firefighters—345,600 career and 814,850 volunteer—for the year 2015).

56. See *Graham v. Connor*, 490 U.S. 386, 396–97 (1989).

57. This document was provided by an agency on the condition of anonymity.

58. This can also be in the form of a letter.

ABOUT THE AUTHOR

Lance J. LoRusso, Esq., a former EMT, began his law enforcement career in 1988 and has been practicing law since 1999. His practice focuses on representing first responders, including when they are injured on and off duty. He represents fire unions and organizations as well as individual firefighters. To date, LoRusso has represented approximately one hundred law enforcement officers involved in on-duty shootings or in-custody deaths. He regularly speaks to and instructs first responders from local, state, federal, and international agencies. His articles and blog posts have been featured in first-responder publications, including *SWAT*, and on websites such as Police One, Law Enforcement Today, and Officer Resource. His first book, *When Cops Kill: The Aftermath of a Critical Incident*, is referenced and used in law enforcement academies and criminal justice programs around the United States. His book *Blue News* addresses the intersection of law enforcement and media. His fiction book *Peacemaking* is a Christian thriller about a cop's walk with Christ, and *Parallax: Crime Tales* is an anthology of short stories. All of his books are available through www.lancelorussobooks.com and Amazon. The profits from his nonfiction books support first-responder charities. His first full-length novel, *Hunting of Men*, is now available at www.huntingofmen.com.

OTHER BOOKS BY
LANCE J. LORUSSO, ESQ.

The World-Class Rainmaker

When Cops Kill

Peacemaking

Blue News

Parallax

Hunting of Men